W9-AXU-609

THE INTERMEDIATE WORLD ATLAS

INCORPORATED

MAPLEWOOD, NEW JERSEY 07040-1396

L. C. 84-80922   ISBN 0-8437-7466-5   PRINTED IN THE UNITED STATES OF AMERICA

Maps updated to 1986

CONTENTS

THE WORLD AND ITS REGIONS

MAPS OF THE WORLD

THE WORLD

Scale at Equator

1000 2000 3000 MI.

0 1000 2000 3000 KM.

© C.S. Hammond & Co.

Longitude West 0° East of Greenwich

NORTH AMERICA
1 ANTIGUA & BARBUDA
  ST. CHRISTOPHER & NEVIS
2 GRENADA, ST. LUCIA,
  ST. VINCENT & GRENS.
3 TRINIDAD & TOBAGO

EUROPE
4 BELGIUM
5 NETHERLANDS
6 WEST GERMANY
7 EAST GERMANY
8 SWITZERLAND
9 AUSTRIA
10 CZECHOSLOVAKIA
11 HUNGARY
12 ALBANIA

AFRICA
13 CAPE VERDE
14 GUINEA-BISSAU
15 SIERRA LEONE
16 IVORY COAST
17 BURKINA FASO
18 BENIN
19 EQUAT. GUINEA
20 SÃO TOMÉ E
   PRÍNCIPE
21 CENT. AFR. REP.
22 UGANDA
23 RWANDA
24 BURUNDI
25 DJIBOUTI

ASIA
26 CYPRUS
27 LEBANON
28 KUWAIT
29 BAHRAIN
30 QATAR
31 YEMEN ARAB REP.
32 UN. ARAB EMIRATES
33 BHUTAN
34 BANGLADESH
35 LAOS
36 SINGAPORE

ARCTIC OCEAN

NORTH PACIFIC OCEAN

UNION OF SOVIET SOCIALIST REPUBLICS

E U R O P E

A S I A

CHINA

MONGOLIA

INDIA

AUSTRALIA

INDONESIA

PHILIPPINES

PAPUA NEW GUINEA

TERR. OF THE PACIFIC ISLANDS (U.S.)

NAURU   KIR.
SOLOMON IS.
TUVALU
VANUATU   FIJI
NEW ZEALAND

INDIAN OCEAN

MADAGASCAR
MAURITIUS
SEYCHELLES
COMOROS
MALDIVES
SRI LANKA

A F R I C A

LIBYA   EGYPT   SUDAN
ALGERIA   NIGER   CHAD
W. SAHARA
MOROCCO
MAURIT.   MALI
SENEGAL
GAMB.
GUINEA
LIBERIA
GHANA   TOGO
CAM.
NIG.
GABON
CONGO   ZAIRE
ANGOLA
NAMIBIA (S.-W. AFRICA)
SOUTH AFRICA
BOTS.
ZIM.
MOZAM.
ZAMBIA
MAL.
TANZANIA
KENYA
ETH.
SOMALIA
SAUDI ARABIA
OMAN
P.D.R. YEMEN
SWAZILAND
LESOTHO

IRAN   IRAQ
AFGH.
PAK.
NEPAL
BURMA
THAI.
CAMB. VIET.
BRUNEI
MALAYSIA
N.KOR.
S.KOR.
TAIWAN
JAPAN

TURKEY   SYR.
ISR. JOR.
BULG. ROM.
YUGO. GR.
ITALY MALTA
SPAIN
PORT.
FINLAND
SWEDEN
NORWAY
DEN.
POL.
FRANCE
UNITED KINGDOM
IRELAND
ICELAND
Arctic Circle

NORTH ATLANTIC OCEAN

GREENLAND (Den.)

CANADA
NORTH AMERICA
UNITED STATES
ALASKA
U.S.

MEXICO
CENTRAL AMERICA
BELIZE GUAT. HON.
EL SAL. NIC.
C.R. PAN.
CUBA JAM.
BAHAMAS
HAITI DOM. REP.
PUERTO RICO
DOMINICA
BARBADOS

COLOMBIA
VENEZUELA
GUYANA SUR. FR. G.
ECU.
PERU
BRAZIL
SOUTH AMERICA
BOL.
PAR.
CHILE
ARGENTINA
URUGUAY

SOUTH ATLANTIC OCEAN

SOUTH PACIFIC OCEAN

KIRIBATI
W. SAMOA
TONGA
HAWAII
U.S.

ANTARCTICA

Antarctic Circle

North Tropic Line (Tropic of Cancer)
South Tropic Line (Tropic of Capricorn)
Equator

3

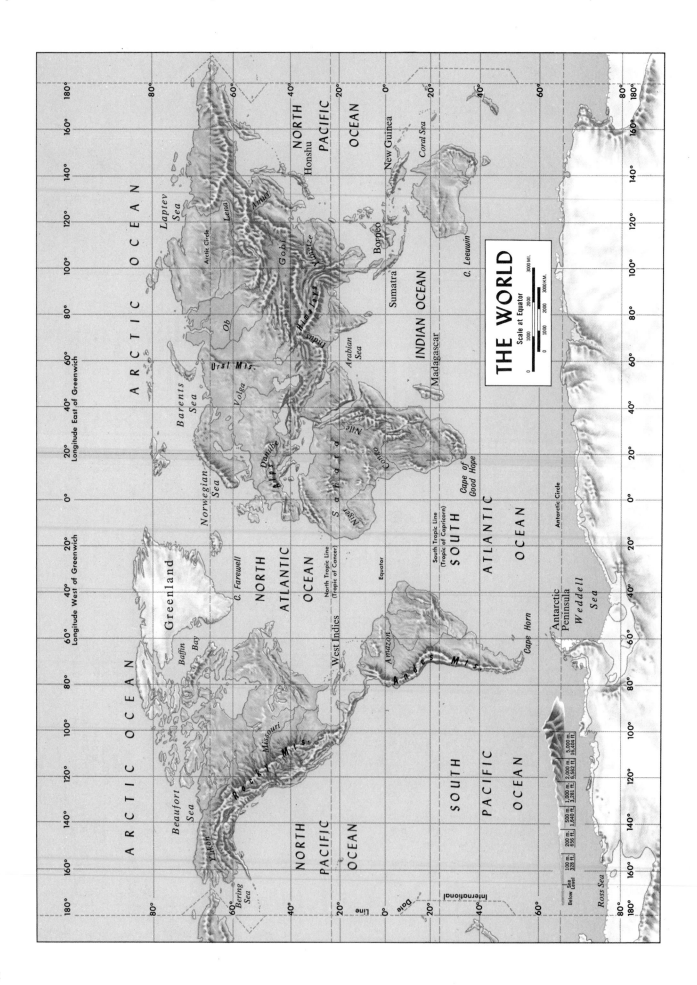

THE WORLD

Scale at Equator

ARCTIC OCEAN

NORTH PACIFIC OCEAN

Laptev Sea

Lena

Amur

Arctic Circle

Gobi

Yangtze

Honshu

NORTH PACIFIC OCEAN

New Guinea

Coral Sea

Borneo

Ob

Himalaya

Indus

Sumatra

INDIAN OCEAN

Ural Mts.

Volga

Arabian Sea

Madagascar

C. Leeuwin

ARCTIC OCEAN

Barents Sea

Longitude East of Greenwich

Danube

Alps

Sahara

Nile

Congo

Norwegian Sea

Niger

Cape of Good Hope

Antarctic Circle

SOUTH ATLANTIC OCEAN

Longitude West of Greenwich

Greenland

C. Farewell

NORTH ATLANTIC OCEAN

North Tropic Line (Tropic of Cancer)

Equator

South Tropic Line (Tropic of Capricorn)

Baffin Bay

West Indies

Amazon

Antarctic Peninsula

Weddell Sea

Missouri

Rocky Mts.

Andes Mts.

Cape Horn

Beaufort Sea

Yukon

Bering Sea

SOUTH PACIFIC OCEAN

NORTH PACIFIC OCEAN

International

Date

Line

Ross Sea

Below Sea Level | Sea Level | 100 m. 328 ft. | 200 m. 656 ft. | 500 m. 1,640 ft. | 1,000 m. 3,281 ft. | 2,000 m. 6,562 ft. | 5,000 m. 16,404 ft.

0   1000   2000   3000 MI.

0   1000   2000   3000 KM.

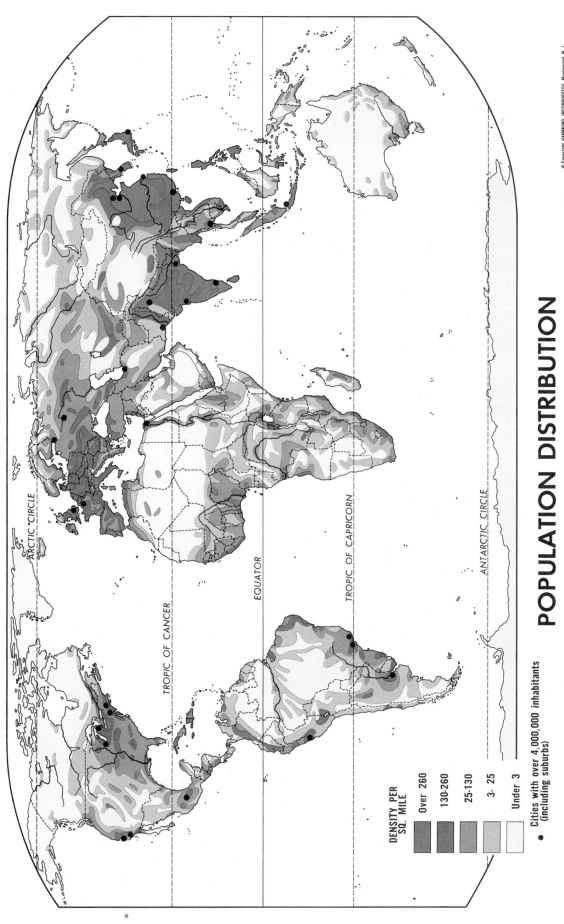

POPULATION DISTRIBUTION

DENSITY PER SQ. MILE

- Over 260
- 130-260
- 25-130
- 3- 25
- Under 3

● Cities with over 4,000,000 inhabitants (including suburbs)

ARCTIC CIRCLE

TROPIC OF CANCER

EQUATOR

TROPIC OF CAPRICORN

ANTARCTIC CIRCLE

© Copyright HAMMOND INCORPORATED, Maplewood, N.J.

Bright

5

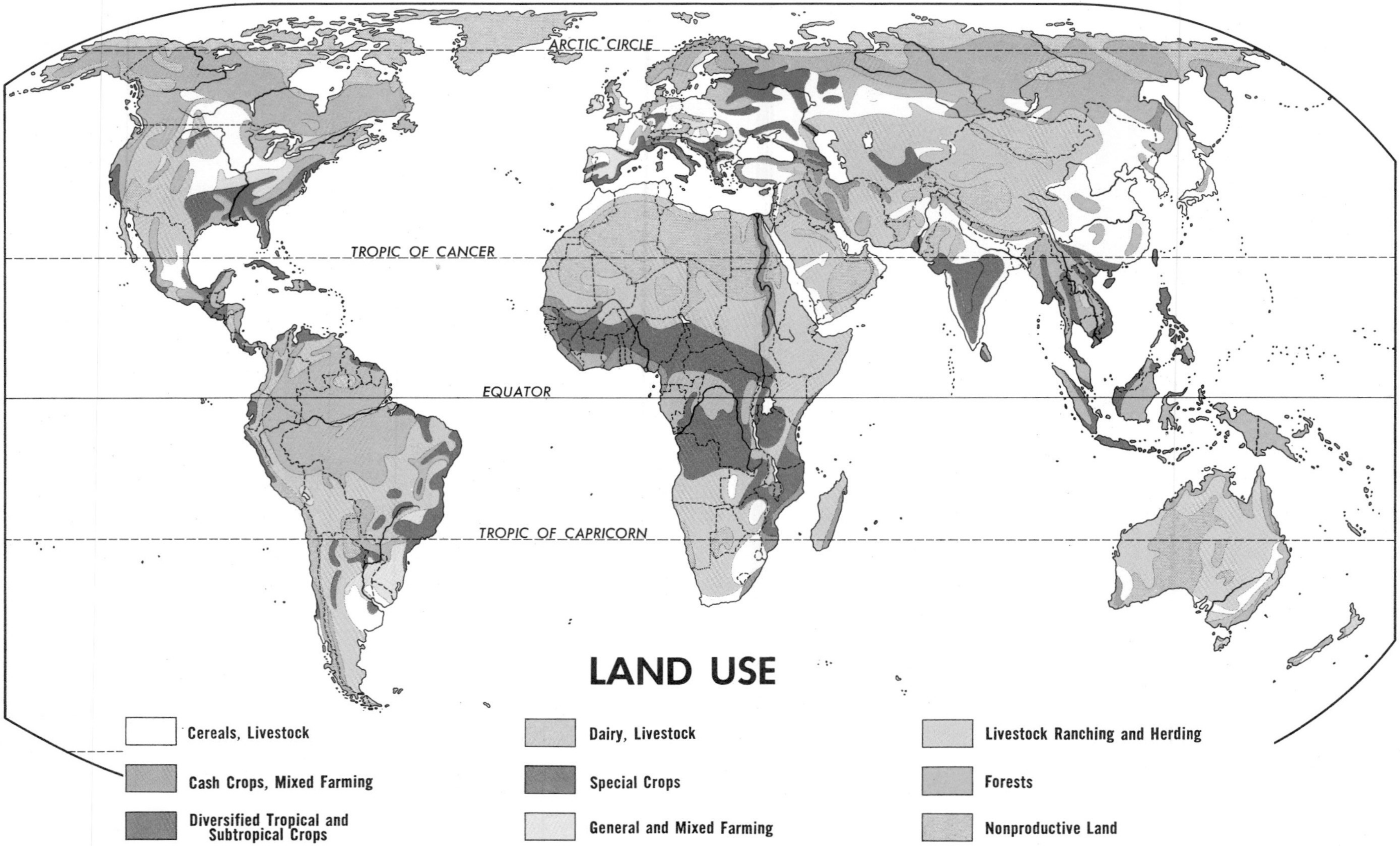

LAND USE

ARCTIC CIRCLE

TROPIC OF CANCER

EQUATOR

TROPIC OF CAPRICORN

Cereals, Livestock

Cash Crops, Mixed Farming

Diversified Tropical and Subtropical Crops

Dairy, Livestock

Special Crops

General and Mixed Farming

Livestock Ranching and Herding

Forests

Nonproductive Land

6

THE WORLD

The earth is our world. It gives us everything we need to live. Yet it is a very small place. The third planet from the sun, the earth is only the fifth largest of the solar system's nine planets in size. The diameter of the earth is about 8,000 miles (13,000 kilometers). Its circumference is almost 25,000 miles (40,000 kilometers).

As far as we know, the earth is the only planet on which there is life. It is also the only one that has any water. If you look at the map of the world on page 4, you will see that the surface of the earth is made up of water and land areas. A little more than 70 percent of the world is water. The remaining part is land.

The great mass of water that covers most of the earth is often called the *world ocean*. It is made up of four major oceans: the Pacific Ocean, which is by far the largest, the Atlantic Ocean, the Indian Ocean, and the Arctic Ocean. The oceans are further subdivided into smaller bodies of water, such as seas, gulfs, and bays.

The floor of the ocean is not smooth. Like land above water, it has high mountains, flat areas, hills, volcanoes, and deep trenches. The greatest known depth of the oceans is located in the Pacific near the island of Guam. Here, Challenger Deep drops more than 36,000 feet (11,000 meters) beneath the rest of the ocean floor.

The remaining bodies of water on earth are inland. The largest inland body of water is the salty Caspian Sea, which is located between Europe and Asia. Although it is called a sea, the Caspian is actually a lake because it has no outlet to the ocean. The largest freshwater lake is Lake Superior in North America. The three longest rivers are, in order of length, the Nile of Africa, the Amazon of South America, and the Mississippi-Missouri of North America.

The oceans and other bodies of water play a very important part in our lives. People cannot live without water. Plants need it to grow. Water areas give us food and other natural resources. They are a source of electric power. They are used for transportation.

The land above water forms seven great landmasses called *continents*. Some scientists believe that about 250 million years ago there was only one giant landmass. This mass, which has been named *Pangaea,* gradually began to break apart. The sections slowly drifted in different directions. Forces within the land and the impact of the ocean water caused the continents to change shape. After millions of years, the landmasses became the seven continents of today. They are, in order of size: Asia, Africa, North America, South America, Antarctica, Europe, and Australia. Europe and Asia are often referred to together as "Eurasia."

In addition to the continents, there are thousands of smaller pieces of land above water. These islands often are near continents. In one place in the Pacific, thousands of islands stretch across the ocean. They are grouped under the name *Oceania.*

The continents differ from each other. Yet they all have the four major kinds of land: smooth lowlands, or plains; raised flatlands, or plateaus; hilly lands; and mountains. Look at the altitude scale on the map. All the areas under 1,600 feet (488 meters) are lowlands. In general, mountains are higher than hills, and they are more rugged and have many individual tall peaks. Different kinds of plants and animals are found at different heights in the mountains. The steep drops, cold temperatures, and high winds in many mountain areas make it difficult to build highways and railways in these regions.

The continents of Africa and Antarctica are mainly plateaus. The other continents have extensive plains or lowlands bordered in part by mountains or hills.

The mountains of the world can be grouped into two great mountain belts. One belt nearly encircles the Pacific Ocean. Starting in Antarctica, these mountains run northward along the west coast of South America and upwards through North America. The mountains then curve through the Aleutian Islands of Alaska and arc southward through the islands off the eastern coast of Asia to end in eastern Australia.

The second major belt centers in the Pamir mountainous region of Asia, just north of Pakistan where Afghanistan, India, the Soviet Union, and China meet. From this central "knot," mountain ranges spread across Asia and Europe in three main arms. One extends north and northeast into China and the Soviet Union. The second group spreads east and southeast to separate China from India. It includes the Himalayas, where Mt. Everest, the highest mountain peak on earth, is located on the border of China and Nepal. This second group blocks the moisture-laden winds from the ocean, to help make the area to the north the "dry heart of Asia." The third branch extends west to Turkey, the southern part of the Soviet Union, and Europe. The Alps are part of this third group.

Throughout history, high mountains have hindered the spread of people and ideas. Nearly all of the world's large cities and densely populated areas are found in the plains, hilly lands, lower slopes of mountains, and in the broad river valleys of the uplands.

---

1. Explain what is meant by the term "continental drift."
2. List seven countries that occupy land north of the Arctic Circle.

NORTH AMERICA

North America is the third largest continent in size, after Asia and Africa. Situated in the northern half of the Western Hemisphere, the continent extends southwards over 5,000 miles (8,000 kilometers). It joins the continent of South America at the very narrow Isthmus of Panama. The section between Mexico and South America is called Central America, and it is often considered to be a subcontinent of North America.

The coastline of North America is very uneven. Great gulfs and bays reach into the mainland. The largest are Hudson Bay in the north, and the Gulf of Mexico and the Gulf of California in the south.

North America's larger islands are in the Arctic Ocean and in the Caribbean Sea. The largest island in the world, Greenland, is in the Arctic and most of it is covered with snow the year round.

Because it extends from the Arctic almost to the equator, North America has striking contrasts in climate. The temperature is always cold in the far north and always hot in the far south. The north is too cold for agriculture and very few people live there. In the Caribbean, the heat is cooled somewhat by ocean breezes. Unfortunately, most of the islands are in the path of hurricane winds, which destroy property and crops every year. The greater part of North America enjoys a temperate climate with warm summers and cold winters. Rainfall varies. There is over 80 inches of rainfall a year along the northwest Pacific coast and in the tropical rainforest areas of Central America and the Caribbean. There are dry areas also. The driest are in the deserts of the southwestern United States and of Mexico. In Death Valley, California, which is the lowest point in North America, there is less than two inches of rain a year.

Look at the map and compare the location of the United States with that of other countries in North America. Not only is it between Asia and Europe, it is also near South America. Its location is favorable for trade in all directions. Goods can be carried easily over inland waterway systems. The Great Lakes between Canada and the United States form the largest connected area of fresh water on earth. (Incidentally, North America has more lakes than any other continent.) The Great Lakes can be reached through the St. Lawrence Seaway—a series of canals, dams, and locks in the St. Lawrence River. South of the Great Lakes is the Mississippi-Missouri river system, which drains the central plains. Along with the Ohio River and about 250 other tributaries, it forms one of the greatest inland waterway systems in the world.

The principal geographical features of North America are its two mountain systems and the great central plains that lie between them. On the west coast, high and rugged mountains extend the entire length of the continent. In the north they begin at the tip of Alaska. The highest peak in North America, Mt. McKinley, is in Alaska. The western mountains include the Coast Ranges that hug the Pacific coast and the Rocky Mountains farther inland. The Rockies extend southward into Mexico, where they are called the Sierra Madre Oriental and the Sierra Madre Occidental. Lying between the Rocky Mountains and the coast ranges are lower areas—basins and plateaus. (A basin is an area that is lower than the surrounding land. It is shaped somewhat like a basin, or bowl.) The largest are the Columbia Plateau, the Colorado Plateau, and the Great Basin. These intermountain areas are dry and have harsh climates, but they are rich in minerals, and their scenery is spectacularly beautiful.

The other mountain system, the Appalachian Mountains, is in the east. This area is a mixture of mountain and plateau and extends from the Gulf of St. Lawrence almost to the Gulf of Mexico. The Appalachians are not very rugged. Their peaks are worn down and rounded. On the east they merge with the Piedmont Plateau, which slopes into the Atlantic Coastal Plain. The Appalachian region is rich in minerals and has many fertile river valleys. The rivers provide abundant water power for the area.

Surrounding Hudson Bay and covering about one-half of Canada is the Laurentian Plateau, or the Canadian Shield. It is a region of rock and poor soil and consists mainly of low-lying hills, rounded mountains, and many lakes. There is little agricultural land here, but the plateau is rich in minerals.

In the middle of North America, between the Rocky Mountains and the Appalachians are the central plains. The plains are shaped like a giant "V" and extend from southern Canada to the Gulf of Mexico. The western part of the region is called the Great Plains. The plains of southern Canada and northern United States are among the most fertile in the world. Other extensive lowlands in North America are in the southeastern United States and on the southeast coast of Mexico. The lowlands in the north are *tundra*—areas where the soil is frozen most of the year and where only a few low plants will grow.

---

1. List the seven countries of Central America.
2. What is the St. Lawrence Seaway? Why is it an important waterway?
3. What is the Canadian Shield?

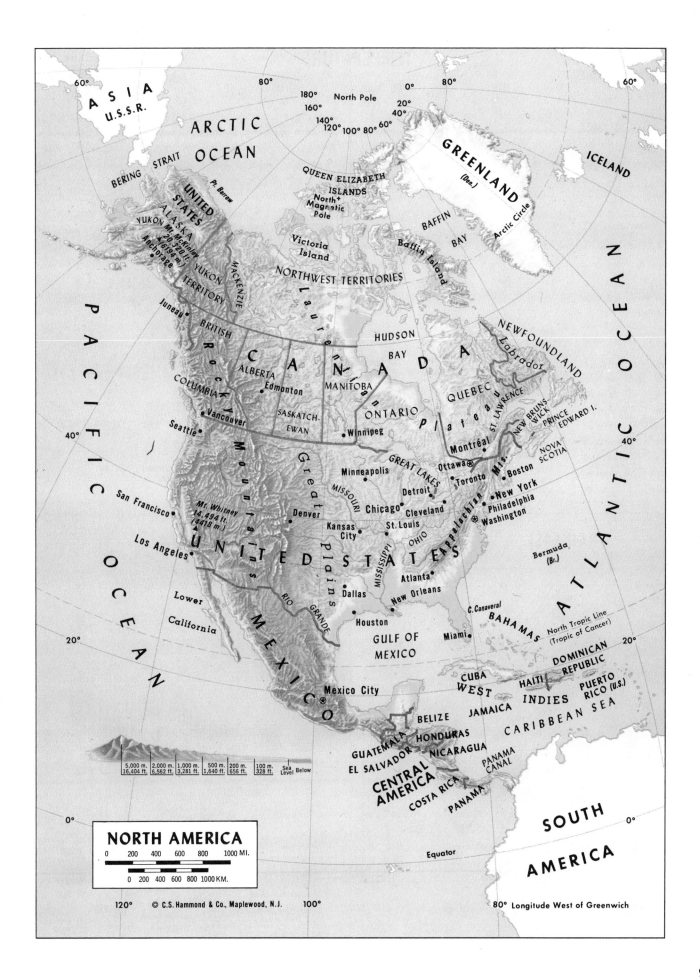

ASIA
U.S.S.R.

ARCTIC OCEAN

60° 80° 0° 80° 60°

180° North Pole 20°
160° 40°
140° 120° 100° 80° 60°

BERING STRAIT

Pt. Barrow

QUEEN ELIZABETH ISLANDS

GREENLAND
(Den.)

ICELAND

UNITED STATES
ALASKA
YUKON Mt. McKinley
20,320 ft.
(6,194 m.)
Anchorage
Juneau

North+ Magnetic Pole

BAFFIN
BAY

Arctic Circle

Victoria Island

Baffin Island

YUKON TERRITORY

MACKENZIE

NORTHWEST TERRITORIES

Laurentian

HUDSON
BAY

NEWFOUNDLAND

Labrador

PACIFIC OCEAN

BRITISH
COLUMBIA

C A N A D A

ROCKY

ALBERTA
Edmonton

SASKATCH-
EWAN

MANITOBA

ONTARIO

QUEBEC

Plateau

ST. LAWRENCE

NEW BRUNS-
WICK
PRINCE
EDWARD I.

40°

Seattle
Vancouver

Great Plains

Winnipeg

GREAT LAKES

Montréal
Ottawa
Toronto

Mtis.
Boston

NOVA SCOTIA

40°

Mountains

Minneapolis

MISSOURI

Detroit
Chicago
Cleveland

Appalachian

New York
Philadelphia
Washington

San Francisco

Mt. Whitney
14,494 ft.
(4418 m.)

Denver

Kansas
City

St. Louis

OHIO

ATLANTIC OCEAN

Los Angeles

U N I T E D   S T A T E S

MISSISSIPPI

Bermuda
(Br.)

Lower
California

RIO
GRANDE

Dallas

Atlanta

New Orleans

C. Canaveral

BAHAMAS

North Tropic Line
(Tropic of Cancer)

Houston

M E X I C O

GULF OF
MEXICO

Miami

20°

20°

CUBA
WEST

HAITI

DOMINICAN
REPUBLIC

PUERTO
RICO (U.S.)

Mexico City

INDIES

BELIZE
GUATEMALA
HONDURAS
EL SALVADOR
NICARAGUA
CENTRAL
AMERICA
COSTA RICA

JAMAICA

CARIBBEAN SEA

PANAMA
CANAL

PANAMA

0°

0°

SOUTH

Equator

AMERICA

5,000 m. 2,000 m. 1,000 m. 500 m. 200 m. 100 m. Sea
16,404 ft. 6,562 ft. 3,281 ft. 1,640 ft. 656 ft. 328 ft. Level Below

NORTH AMERICA
0   200   400   600   800   1000 MI.
0   200 400 600 800 1000 KM.

120°   © C.S. Hammond & Co., Maplewood, N.J.   100°   80° Longitude West of Greenwich

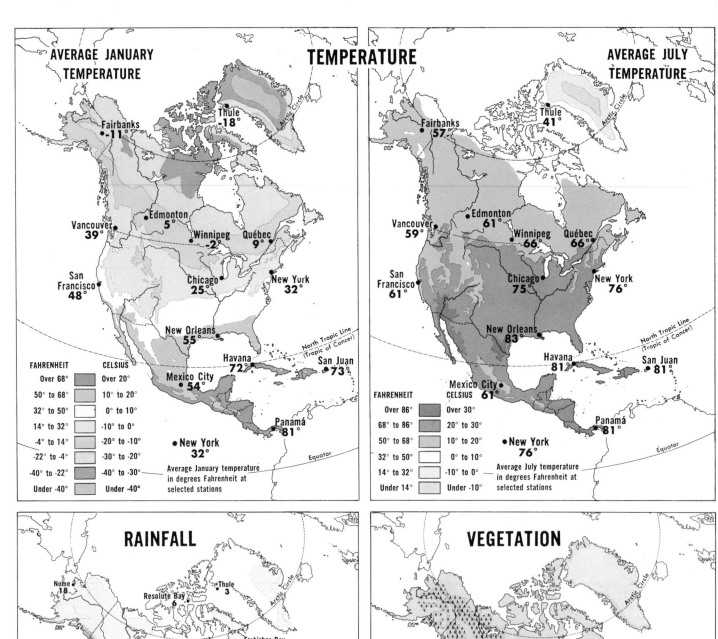

TEMPERATURE

AVERAGE JANUARY TEMPERATURE

Thule -18°
Fairbanks -11°
Vancouver 39°
Edmonton 5°
Winnipeg -2°
Québec 9°
San Francisco 48°
Chicago 25°
New York 32°
New Orleans 55°
Havana 72°
San Juan 73°
Mexico City 54°
Panamá 81°

FAHRENHEIT	CELSIUS
Over 68°	Over 20°
50° to 68°	10° to 20°
32° to 50°	0° to 10°
14° to 32°	-10° to 0°
-4° to 14°	-20° to -10°
-22° to -4°	-30° to -20°
-40° to -22°	-40° to -30°
Under -40°	Under -40°

North Tropic Line (Tropic of Cancer)
Equator

● New York 32°

Average January temperature in degrees Fahrenheit at selected stations

AVERAGE JULY TEMPERATURE

Thule 41°
Fairbanks 57°
Vancouver 59°
Edmonton 61°
Winnipeg 66°
Québec 66°
San Francisco 61°
Chicago 75°
New York 76°
New Orleans 83°
Havana 81°
San Juan 81°
Mexico City 61°
Panamá 81°

FAHRENHEIT	CELSIUS
Over 86°	Over 30°
68° to 86°	20° to 30°
50° to 68°	10° to 20°
32° to 50°	0° to 10°
14° to 32°	-10° to 0°
Under 14°	Under -10°

North Tropic Line (Tropic of Cancer)
Equator

● New York 76°

Average July temperature in degrees Fahrenheit at selected stations

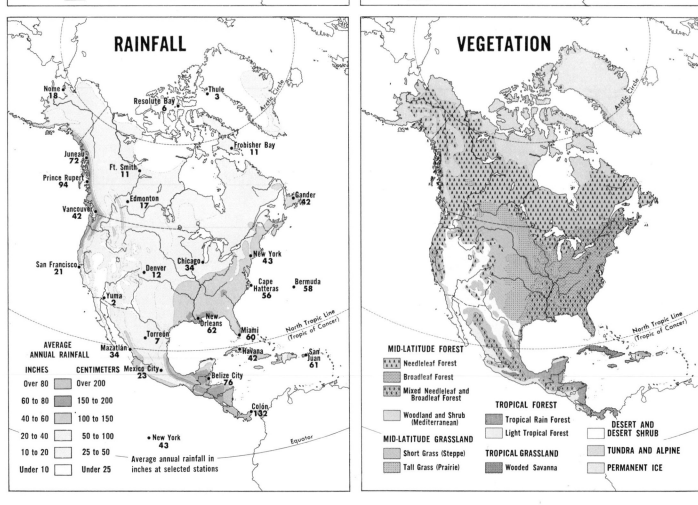

RAINFALL

Nome 18
Thule 3
Resolute Bay 6
Frobisher Bay 11
Juneau 72
Ft. Smith 11
Prince Rupert 94
Vancouver 42
Edmonton 17
Gander 42
San Francisco 21
Denver 12
Chicago 34
New York 43
Yuma 2
Cape Hatteras 56
Bermuda 58
New Orleans 62
Torreón 7
Miami 60
Mazatlán 34
Havana 42
San Juan 61
Mexico City 23
Belize City 76
Colón 132

North Tropic Line (Tropic of Cancer)
Equator

AVERAGE ANNUAL RAINFALL

INCHES	CENTIMETERS
Over 80	Over 200
60 to 80	150 to 200
40 to 60	100 to 150
20 to 40	50 to 100
10 to 20	25 to 50
Under 10	Under 25

● New York 43

Average annual rainfall in inches at selected stations

VEGETATION

North Tropic Line (Tropic of Cancer)

MID-LATITUDE FOREST
- Needleleaf Forest
- Broadleaf Forest
- Mixed Needleleaf and Broadleaf Forest
- Woodland and Shrub (Mediterranean)

MID-LATITUDE GRASSLAND
- Short Grass (Steppe)
- Tall Grass (Prairie)

TROPICAL FOREST
- Tropical Rain Forest
- Light Tropical Forest

TROPICAL GRASSLAND
- Wooded Savanna

DESERT AND DESERT SHRUB
- Desert and Desert Shrub
- Tundra and Alpine
- Permanent Ice

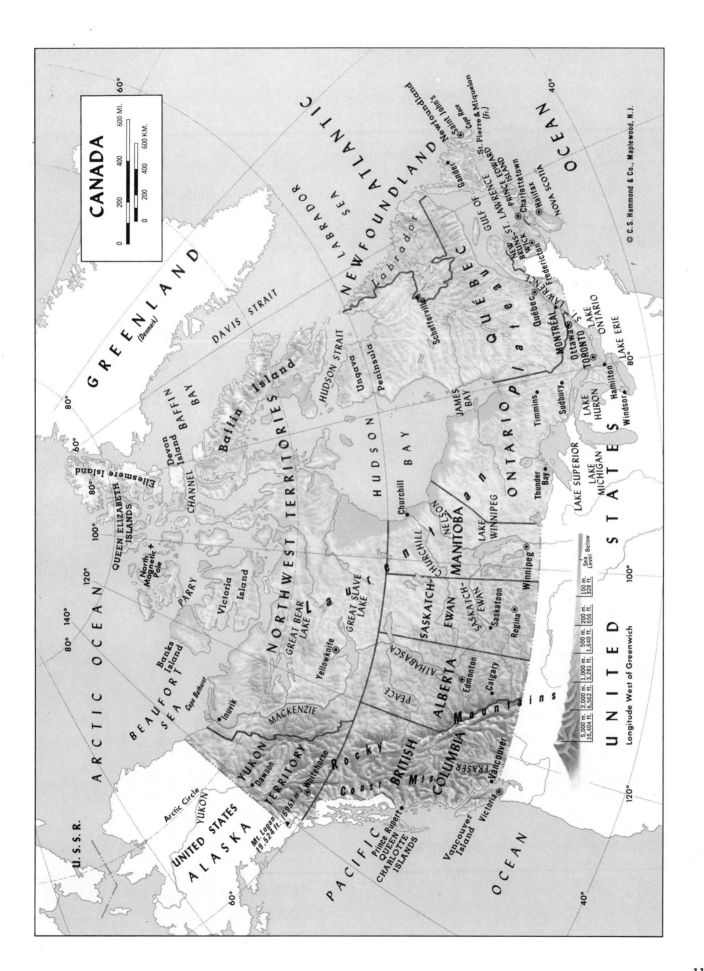

CANADA

600 MI.
400
200
0

600 KM.
400
200
0

© C.S. Hammond & Co., Maplewood, N.J.

GREENLAND
(Denmark)

DAVIS STRAIT

BAFFIN BAY

Devon Island

Baffin Island

Ellesmere Island

QUEEN ELIZABETH ISLANDS

North Magnetic Pole

CHANNEL

PARRY

Banks Island

Victoria Island

BEAUFORT SEA

ARCTIC OCEAN

Cape Bathurst

Inuvik

MACKENZIE

NORTHWEST TERRITORIES

Great Bear Lake

Great Slave Lake

Yellowknife

U.S.S.R.

UNITED STATES
ALASKA

YUKON TERRITORY

Dawson

Whitehorse

Arctic Circle

YUKON

Mt Logan 19,524 ft. (5,951 m.)

Rocky Mountains

Coast Mts.

BRITISH COLUMBIA

FRASER

Prince Rupert

QUEEN CHARLOTTE ISLANDS

Vancouver Island

Victoria

Vancouver

PACIFIC OCEAN

ALBERTA

PEACE

ATHABASCA

Edmonton

Calgary

SASKATCH-EWAN

Saskatoon

Regina

NELSON

CHURCHILL

Churchill

MANITOBA

Winnipeg

LAKE WINNIPEG

HUDSON BAY

JAMES BAY

Ungava Peninsula

HUDSON STRAIT

LABRADOR

Labrador

NEWFOUNDLAND

LABRADOR SEA

ATLANTIC OCEAN

QUÉBEC

Ontario Plateau

Schefferville

St. John's

Cape Race

Gander

Newfoundland

St. Pierre & Miquelon (Fr.)

GULF OF ST. LAWRENCE

PRINCE EDWARD ISLAND

Charlottetown

NEW BRUNS-WICK

Fredericton

NOVA SCOTIA

Halifax

ST. LAWRENCE

Québec

Montréal

Ottawa

TORONTO

LAKE ONTARIO

LAKE ERIE

Hamilton

Windsor

Sudbury

Timmins

Thunder Bay

LAKE SUPERIOR

LAKE HURON

LAKE MICHIGAN

UNITED STATES

Longitude West of Greenwich

Sea Below Level
100 m. 328 ft.
200 m. 656 ft.
500 m. 1,640 ft.
1,000 m. 3,281 ft.
2,000 m. 6,562 ft.
5,000 m. 16,404 ft.

40°

60°

80°

100°

120°

140°

80°

60°

40°

11

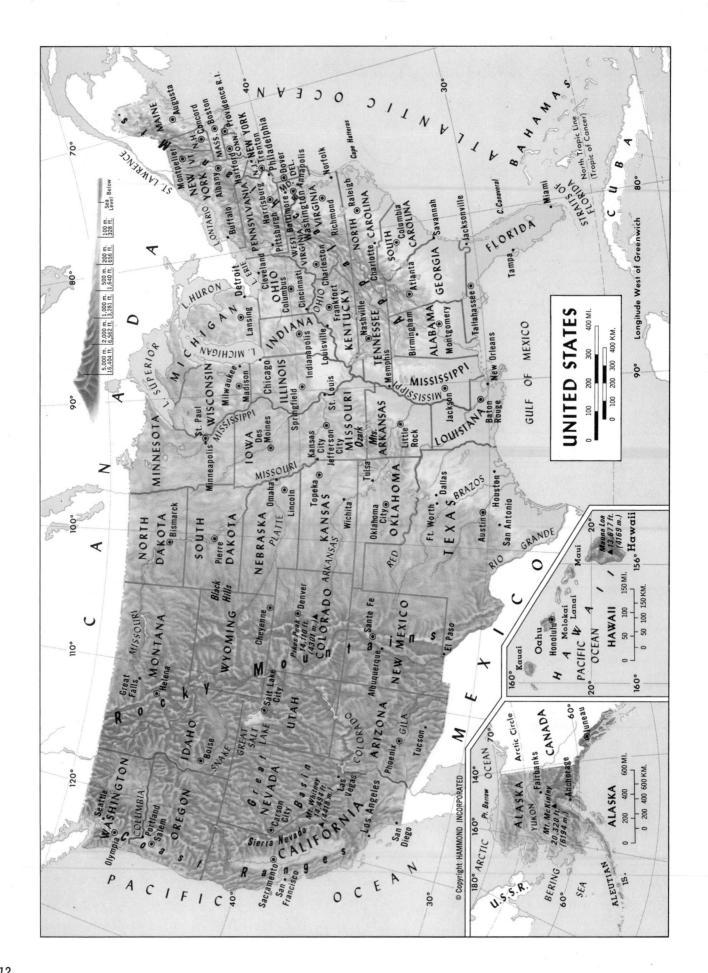

UNITED STATES

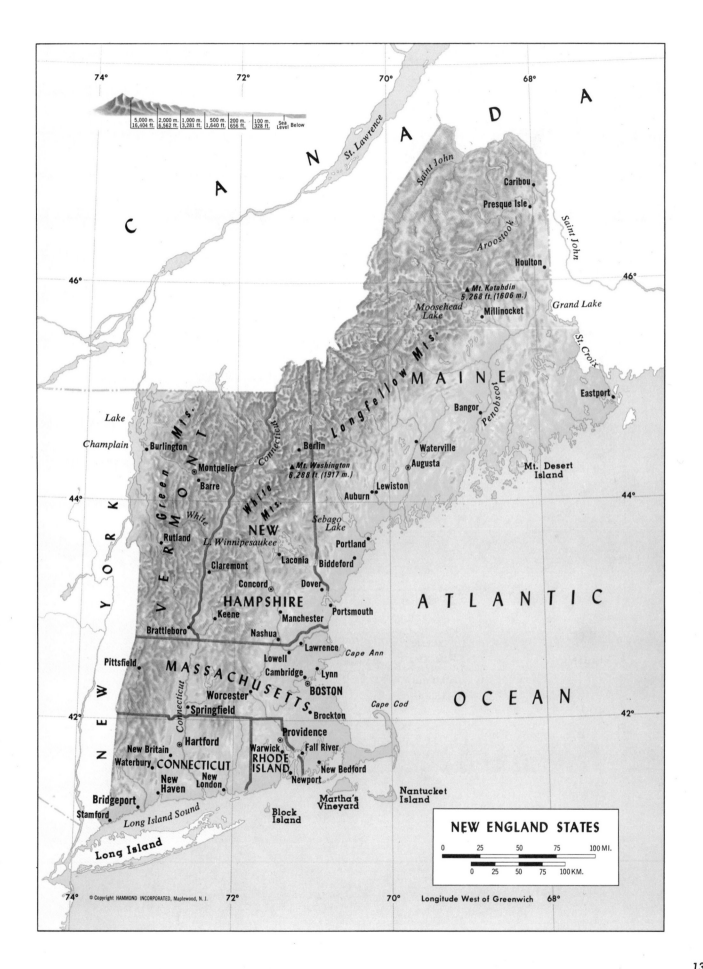

74° 72° 70° 68°

5,000 m. 2,000 m. 1,000 m. 500 m. 200 m. 100 m. Sea Below
16,404 ft. 6,562 ft. 3,281 ft. 1,640 ft. 656 ft. 328 ft. Level

C A N A D A

St. Lawrence

Saint John

Caribou

Presque Isle

Aroostook

Saint John

Houlton

46° 46°

▲ Mt. Katahdin
5,268 ft. (1606 m.)

Grand Lake

Moosehead Lake

Millinocket

St. Croix

Longfellow M A I N E

Eastport

Longfellow Mts.

Bangor

Penobscot

Lake

Champlain

Burlington

Berlin

Waterville

Mt. Desert Island

Montpelier

Connecticut

⊚ Augusta

Barre

▲ Mt. Washington
6,288 ft. (1917 m.)

Lewiston

44° Rutland *White* Auburn 44°

White Mts.

Sebago Lake

NEW

L. Winnipesaukee

Claremont

Laconia

Portland

Biddeford

Concord Dover

HAMPSHIRE

Portsmouth

Keene

Manchester

Brattleboro

Nashua

A T L A N T I C

Pittsfield

Lawrence *Cape Ann*

M A S S A C H U S E T T S

Lowell

Cambridge Lynn

O C E A N

Connecticut

Worcester ⊚ BOSTON

Springfield

Brockton *Cape Cod*

42° 42°

Hartford

Providence

New Britain Warwick Fall River

Waterbury CONNECTICUT RHODE ISLAND

New Bedford

New New Newport
Haven London

Nantucket Island

Bridgeport

Martha's Vineyard

Stamford

Long Island Sound

Block Island

Long Island

© Copyright HAMMOND INCORPORATED, Maplewood, N.J. 72° 70° Longitude West of Greenwich 68°

74°

NEW ENGLAND STATES

0 25 50 75 100 MI.

0 25 50 75 100 KM.

V E R M O N T

Green Mts.

N E W Y O R K

13

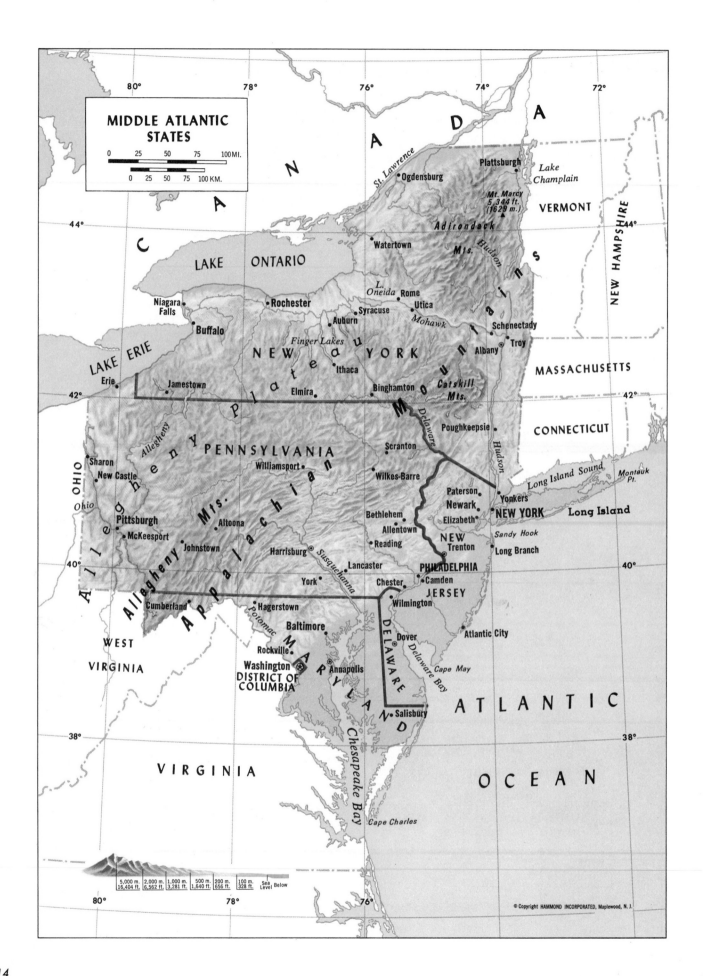

MIDDLE ATLANTIC STATES

0 25 50 75 100 MI.

0 25 50 75 100 KM.

C A N A D A

CANADA

80° 78° 76° 74° 72°

44° 44°

42° 42°

40° 40°

38° 38°

LAKE ONTARIO

LAKE ERIE

St. Lawrence • Ogdensburg

Plattsburgh   *Lake Champlain*

Mt. Marcy 5,344 ft. (1629 m.) ▲

Adirondack VERMONT

Watertown

Mts. *Hudson*

NEW HAMPSHIRE

Niagara Falls

• Rochester

L. Oneida Rome

Syracuse • Utica

Auburn *Mohawk* Schenectady • Troy

Buffalo

Finger Lakes

N E W *Plateau* Y O R K

Albany

MASSACHUSETTS

Erie •

• Jamestown

Ithaca

Elmira •

Binghamton • *Catskill Mts.*

Delaware

Poughkeepsie

Hudson

CONNECTICUT

Allegheny

PENNSYLVANIA

Scranton •

M o u n t a i n s

Sharon •

New Castle •

Williamsport •

Wilkes-Barre •

Paterson • Newark •

Long Island Sound

Montauk Pt.

OHIO

Allegheny

Mts.

Bethlehem •

Elizabeth •

Yonkers

Pittsburgh •

Altoona •

Allentown •

NEW YORK

Long Island

Ohio

McKeesport •

Johnstown •

A p p a l a c h i a n

Harrisburg ⊛

Susquehanna

Reading •

Lancaster •

NEW

Trenton ⊙

Sandy Hook

Long Branch •

PHILADELPHIA

York •

Chester • Camden •

JERSEY

Cumberland •

• Hagerstown

Potomac

Wilmington •

Atlantic City •

WEST

VIRGINIA

Rockville •

Baltimore •

M A R Y L A N D

DELAWARE

Dover ⊙

Delaware Bay

Washington ⊛

DISTRICT OF COLUMBIA

Annapolis ⊙

Cape May

VIRGINIA

Chesapeake Bay

Salisbury •

A T L A N T I C

O C E A N

Cape Charles

5,000 m. 2,000 m. 1,000 m. 500 m. 200 m. 100 m. Sea Below
16,404 ft. 6,562 ft. 3,281 ft. 1,640 ft. 656 ft. 328 ft. Level

80° 78° 76°

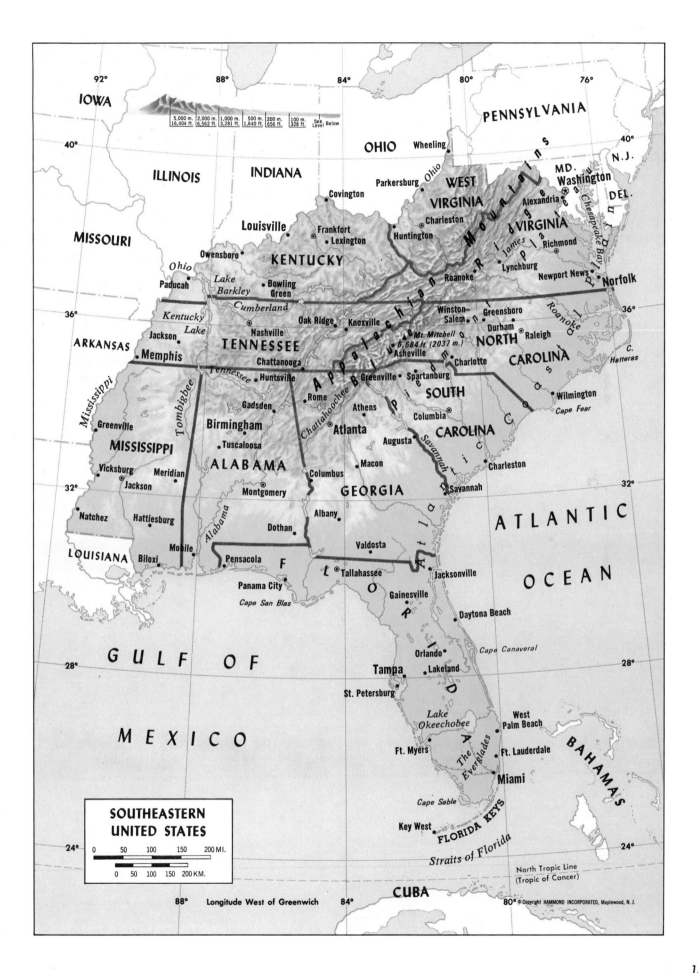

IOWA

92°

88°

84°

80°

76°

OHIO · Wheeling
ILLINOIS
INDIANA
PENNSYLVANIA
40°
40°

Parkersburg · Ohio
· Covington
WEST
VIRGINIA
MD.
Washington
N.J.
DEL.

Louisville · Frankfort
Lexington
· Charleston
· Huntington
Alexandria
VIRGINIA
Chesapeake Bay

MISSOURI
Owensboro ·
KENTUCKY
Roanoke ·
James
· Richmond
Lynchburg
Newport News
Norfolk

Ohio
· Paducah
Lake
Barkley
· Bowling
Green
Cumberland
Winston-
Salem
· Greensboro
Roanoke
36°
36°

Kentucky
Lake
Oak Ridge · Knoxville
Durham · Raleigh
Jackson ·
Nashville
· Mt. Mitchell
6,684 ft. (2037 m.)
NORTH
C.
Hatteras

ARKANSAS
· Memphis
TENNESSEE
Asheville
Charlotte
CAROLINA

Mississippi
Tennessee
· Chattanooga
Huntsville
Greenville
· Spartanburg
SOUTH

Rome
Athens
· Columbia
Wilmington
Cape Fear

Greenville ·
Tombigbee
Gadsden ·
CAROLINA
Charleston

Birmingham
· Atlanta
Augusta
Chattahoochee
Savannah

MISSISSIPPI
· Tuscaloosa
· Macon
32°
32°

Vicksburg ·
Meridian ·
ALABAMA
Columbus ·
GEORGIA
Savannah
ATLANTIC

Jackson
Alabama
Montgomery ·
Albany ·

Natchez ·
Hattiesburg ·
Dothan ·
OCEAN

LOUISIANA
Mobile ·
Pensacola
F
Valdosta ·

Biloxi
Panama City
Cape San Blas
L
· Tallahassee
Jacksonville

Gainesville ·

O
Daytona Beach

GULF OF
R
Cape Canaveral
28°
28°

Orlando ·
Lakeland
Tampa ·

St. Petersburg ·
D

MEXICO
Lake
Okeechobee
West
Palm Beach

Ft. Myers ·
The
Everglades
· Ft. Lauderdale

A
· Miami

Cape Sable
BAHAMAS

Key West
FLORIDA KEYS
Straits of Florida
24°
24°

SOUTHEASTERN
UNITED STATES
North Tropic Line
(Tropic of Cancer)

0   50   100   150   200 MI.

0   50   100 150 200 KM.

88°
Longitude West of Greenwich
84°
CUBA
80° © Copyright HAMMOND INCORPORATED, Maplewood, N.J.

5,000 m.
16,404 ft.
2,000 m.
6,562 ft.
1,000 m.
3,281 ft.
500 m.
1,640 ft.
200 m.
656 ft.
100 m.
328 ft.
Sea
Level
Below

15

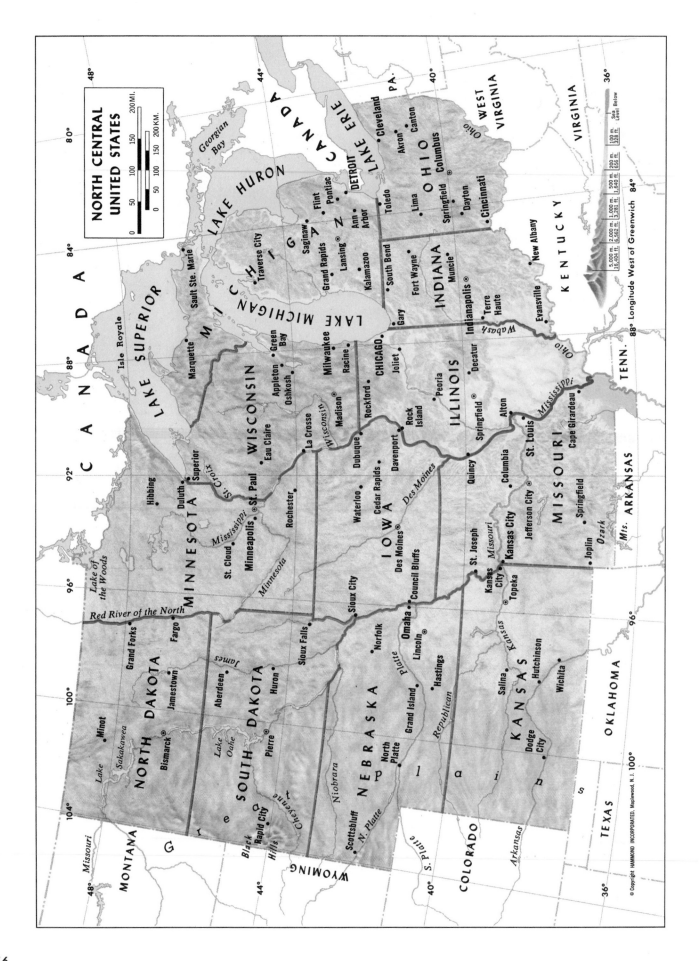

NORTH CENTRAL
UNITED STATES

CANADA

Georgian
Bay

LAKE HURON

Sault Ste. Marie

LAKE SUPERIOR

Isle Royale

M I C H I G A N

DETROIT
LAKE ERIE
PA.

Cleveland • Canton
Akron •
• Columbus
O H I O
Springfield • Dayton
Cincinnati •

WEST
VIRGINIA

VIRGINIA

Traverse City
Saginaw • Flint • Pontiac
Grand Rapids Ann
Lansing ◉ Arbor
Kalamazoo
South Bend •
Fort Wayne •
Muncie
I N D I A N A
Indianapolis ◉
Gary Terre
Haute
New Albany
Evansville •

K E N T U C K Y

L A K E   M I C H I G A N

Marquette •

W I S C O N S I N

Green
Bay
Appleton •
Oshkosh •
Milwaukee
Racine
CHICAGO
Joliet
Rockford
Peoria •
I L L I N O I S
Decatur •
Springfield ◉

Ohio

Wabash

Ohio

TENN.

Isle Royale

Superior •
Hibbing •
Duluth •

St. Croix

St. Paul ◉
Minneapolis ◉

Madison ◉

La Crosse •

Wisconsin

Eau Claire •

Dubuque •
Davenport
Rock Island

Rock
Island

Quincy •

Alton •
St. Louis •
Cape Girardeau •

Mississippi

M I N N E S O T A

St. Cloud •

Rochester •

Mississippi

Minnesota

Des Moines

I O W A

Waterloo •
Cedar Rapids •

Columbia •
Jefferson City ◉

M I S S O U R I

Springfield •

Ozark

Mts. ARKANSAS

Lake
of the Woods

Red River of the North

Grand Forks •
Fargo •

Jamestown •
N O R T H   D A K O T A
Bismarck ◉
Minot •

Lake
Sakakawea

James

Aberdeen •
Huron •
S O U T H   D A K O T A
Pierre ◉

Lake
Oahe

Sioux Falls •

Sioux City •
Council Bluffs •
Des Moines ◉

Omaha •
Lincoln ◉

St. Joseph •
Kansas City

Missouri

Kansas City
Topeka ◉
Kansas

Joplin •

Norfolk •
Hastings •
Grand Island •
N E B R A S K A

P   l   a   i   n   s

Kansas

Salina •
Hutchinson •
Wichita •
K A N S A S
Dodge
City •

Republican

Niobrara

North Platte •
N. Platte

Platte

CANADA

Black
Hills

Rapid City •

Cheyenne

Scottsbluff •
N. Platte

S. Platte

Missouri

MONTANA

G r e a t

WYOMING

COLORADO

Arkansas

TEXAS

OKLAHOMA

88° Longitude West of Greenwich   84°

100 m.   200 m.   500 m.   1,000 m.   2,000 m.   5,000 m.
328 ft.   656 ft.   1,640 ft.   3,281 ft.   6,562 ft.   16,404 ft.

Sea   Below
Level

100°   96°

© Copyright HAMMOND INCORPORATED, Maplewood, N.J.

0   50   100   150   200 MI.
0   50   100   150   200 KM.

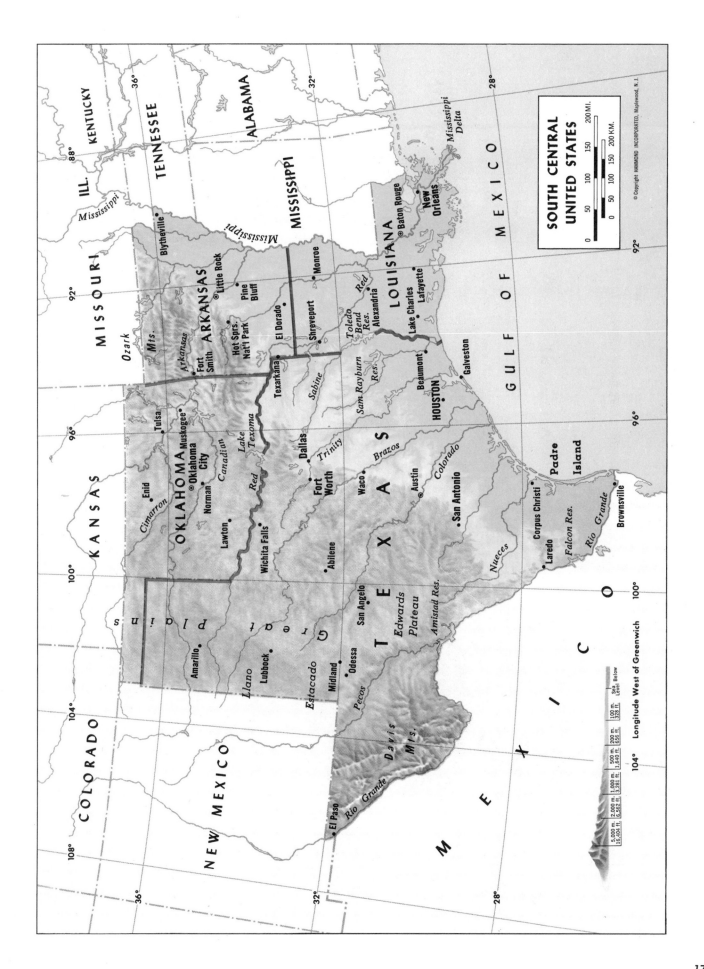

SOUTH CENTRAL
UNITED STATES

© Copyright HAMMOND INCORPORATED, Maplewood, N.J.

200 MI.

200 KM.

150

100

50

0

Longitude West of Greenwich

5,000 m. 2,000 m. 1,000 m. 500 m. 200 m. 100 m. Sea Below
16,404 ft. 6,562 ft. 3,281 ft. 1,640 ft. 656 ft. 328 ft. Level

KENTUCKY

ILL.

TENNESSEE

ALABAMA

MISSISSIPPI

MISSOURI

Mississippi

Blytheville

ARKANSAS

Little Rock

Pine Bluff

Ozark Mts.

Arkansas

Hot Sprs.
Nat'l Park

Fort
Smith

El Dorado

Shreveport

Monroe

Red

Toledo
Bend
Res.

Alexandria

Lake Charles

Lafayette

LOUISIANA

Baton Rouge

New Orleans

Mississippi
Delta

GULF OF MEXICO

Texarkana

Sabine

Sam Rayburn
Res.

Beaumont

HOUSTON

Galveston

Tulsa

Muskogee

Lake
Texoma

Canadian

Red

Trinity

Brazos

Colorado

OKLAHOMA

Oklahoma
City

Norman

Dallas

Fort
Worth

Waco

Austin

San Antonio

Padre
Island

Corpus Christi

KANSAS

Enid

Cimarron

Lawton

Wichita Falls

Abilene

T E X A S

San Angelo

Edwards
Plateau

Amistad Res.

Nueces

Laredo

Falcon Res.

Rio Grande

Brownsville

Amarillo

Lubbock

Midland

Odessa

Llano
Estacado

Great
Plains

Pecos

Davis
Mts.

Rio Grande

El Paso

NEW MEXICO

COLORADO

M E X I C O

17

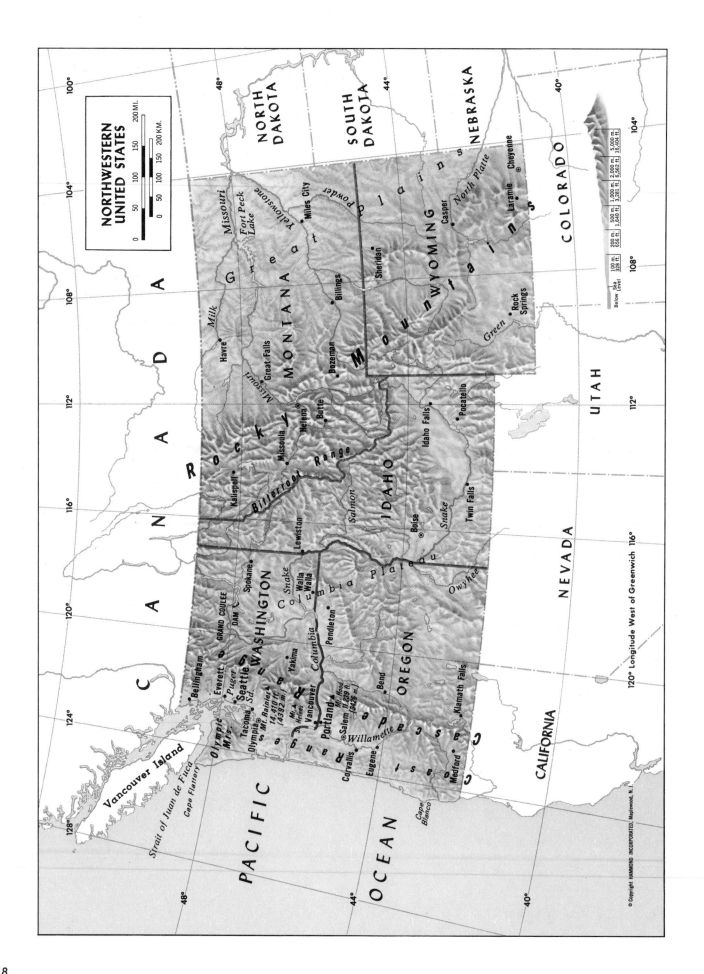

NORTHWESTERN
UNITED STATES

200 MI.
150
100
50
0

200 KM.
150
100
50
0

CANADA

NORTH DAKOTA

SOUTH DAKOTA

NEBRASKA

COLORADO

100°

104°

108°

112°

116°

120°

124°

128°

48°

44°

40°

Missouri
Fort Peck
Lake
Yellowstone
Miles City
Powder
Great
Plains
Sheridan
Cheyenne
Laramie
Casper
North Platte
Rock Springs
Green

Milk
Havre
Great Falls
MONTANA
Billings
WYOMING
Mountains

Missouri
Kalispell
Missoula
Helena
Butte
Bozeman
Bitterroot Range
Salmon
IDAHO
Idaho Falls
Pocatello
Twin Falls
Snake
Boise
Owyhee

ROCKY

Spokane
Snake
Walla Walla
Columbia Plateau
Pendleton
Columbia
Bend
OREGON
Klamath Falls

GRAND COULEE
DAM
WASHINGTON
Bellingham
Everett
Puget Sd.
Seattle
Tacoma
Olympia
Yakima
Mt. Rainier
14,410 ft.
(4392 m.)
Mt. St. Helens
Vancouver
Portland
Mt. Hood
11,239 ft.
(3426 m.)
Salem
Willamette
Corvallis
Eugene
Medford

Olympic Mts.
Cascade
Range
Coast Range

UTAH

NEVADA

CALIFORNIA

120° Longitude West of Greenwich 116°

Vancouver Island
Strait of Juan de Fuca
Cape Flattery

PACIFIC

OCEAN

Cape Blanco

100 m.
328 ft.
Below Sea Level

200 m.
656 ft.
500 m.
1,640 ft.
1,000 m.
3,281 ft.
2,000 m.
6,562 ft.
5,000 m.
16,404 ft.

104°

108°

112°

48°

44°

40°

© Copyright HAMMOND INCORPORATED, Maplewood, N.J.

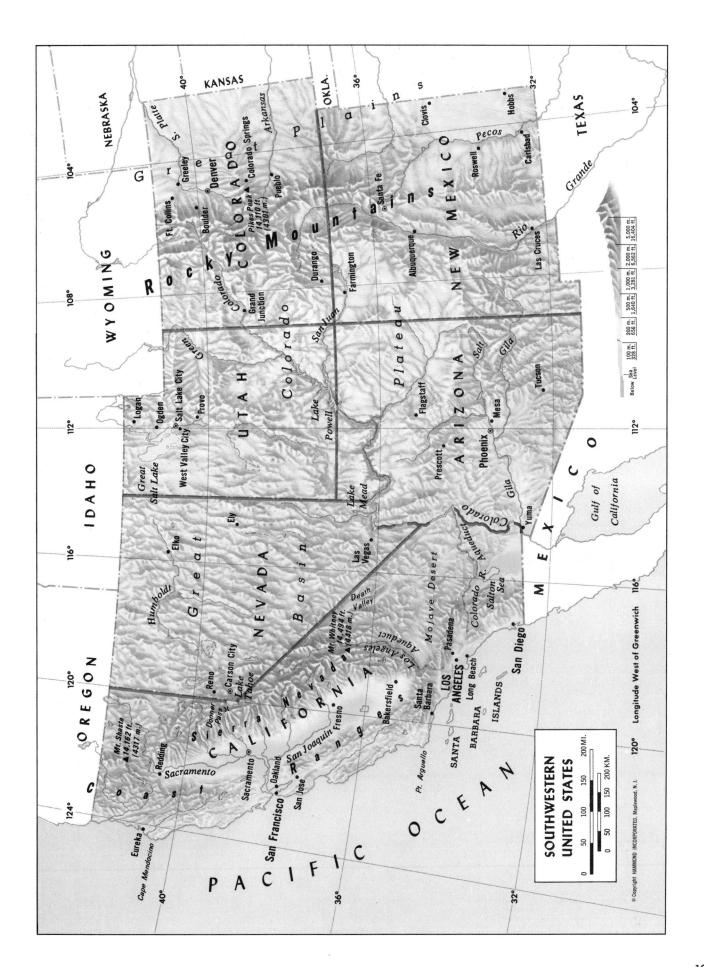

NEBRASKA

KANSAS

OKLA.

TEXAS

40°

36°

32°

104°

108°

112°

116°

120°

124°

WYOMING

IDAHO

OREGON

C   o   a   s   t

Cape Mendocino

Eureka

Redding

Mt. Shasta
▲14,162 ft.
(4317 m.)

Sacramento

San Francisco

Oakland

San Jose

CALIFORNIA

S i e r r a

Donner
Pass

Nevada

R a n g e

San Joaquin

Fresno

Bakersfield

Santa
Barbara

SANTA
BARBARA
ISLANDS

Pt. Arguello

LOS
ANGELES

Pasadena

Long Beach

San Diego

Los Angeles Aqueduct

Death
Valley

Mt. Whitney
14,494 ft.
(4418 m.)

Mojave Desert

NEVADA

G   r   e   a   t

B   a   s   i   n

Reno

Carson City

Lake
Tahoe

Ely

Elko

Humboldt

Las
Vegas

Lake
Mead

Colorado R. Aqueduct

Colorado

Salton
Sea

Yuma

Gila

Gila

Phoenix

Mesa

Prescott

Flagstaff

Tucson

ARIZONA

Salt

MEXICO

Gulf of
California

Great
Salt Lake

Logan

Ogden

Salt Lake City

Provo

West Valley City

UTAH

Green

Colorado

Lake
Powell

C   o   l   o   r   a   d   o

P   l   a   t   e   a   u

San Juan

Colorado

Grand
Junction

Durango

Farmington

COLORADO

R   o   c   k   y

Ft. Collins

Boulder

Greeley

Denver

Colorado Springs

Pikes Peak
14,110 ft.
(4301 m.)

Pueblo

S. Platte

Arkansas

G   r   e   a   t

P   l   a   i   n   s

M   o   u   n   t   a   i   n   s

NEW   MEXICO

Santa Fe

Albuquerque

Las Cruces

Roswell

Clovis

Hobbs

Carlsbad

Pecos

Rio

Grande

Rio Grande

M   E   X   I   C   O

Longitude West of Greenwich

PACIFIC   OCEAN

40°

36°

32°

104°

112°

116°

120°

5,000 m.
16,404 ft.

2,000 m.
6,562 ft.

1,000 m.
3,281 ft.

500 m.
1,640 ft.

200 m.
656 ft.

100 m.
328 ft.

Below   Sea
Level

SOUTHWESTERN
UNITED STATES

200 MI.
150
100
50
0

200 KM.
150
100
50
0

© Copyright HAMMOND INCORPORATED, Maplewood, N.J.

19

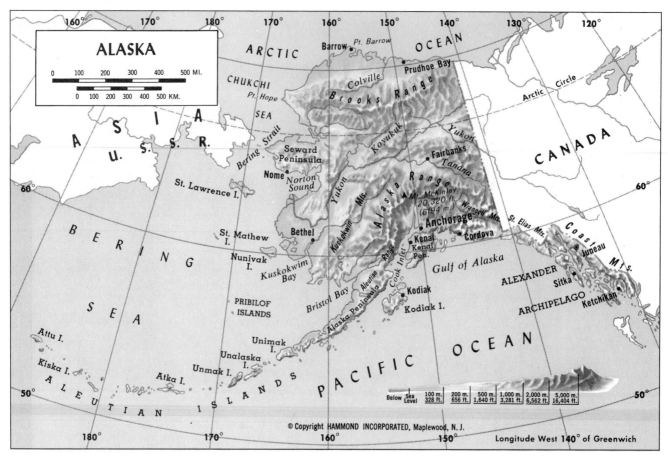

ALASKA

0 100 200 300 400 500 MI.

0 100 200 300 400 500 KM.

ARCTIC OCEAN

Barrow • Pt. Barrow

CHUKCHI

Pt. Hope

SEA

Colville

• Prudhoe Bay

Brooks Range

Arctic Circle

CANADA

Bering Strait

Seward
Peninsula

Koyukuk

Yukon

Nome

Norton
Sound

Yukon

• Fairbanks

Tanana

St. Lawrence I.

Alaska Range

▲ Mt. McKinley
20,320 ft.
(6194 m)

Wrangell Mts.

St. Elias Mts.

Coast

60°

St. Mathew
I.

Kuskokwim

• Anchorage

Cordova

Bethel

Range

• Kenai
Kenai
Pen.

Juneau

Nunivak
I.

Kuskokwim
Bay

Cook Inlet

Gulf of Alaska

Mts.

PRIBILOF
ISLANDS

Bristol Bay

Aleutian

• Kodiak

ALEXANDER

Sitka

BERING

Alaska Peninsula

Range

Kodiak I.

ARCHIPELAGO

Ketchikan

SEA

Attu I.

Unimak
I.

Unalaska
I.

PACIFIC OCEAN

Kiska I.

Unmak I.

Atka I.

ALEUTIAN ISLANDS

| Below Sea Level | 100 m. 328 ft. | 200 m. 656 ft. | 500 m. 1,640 ft. | 1,000 m. 3,281 ft. | 2,000 m. 6,562 ft. | 5,000 m. 16,404 ft. |

50°

© Copyright HAMMOND INCORPORATED, Maplewood, N.J.

Longitude West 140° of Greenwich

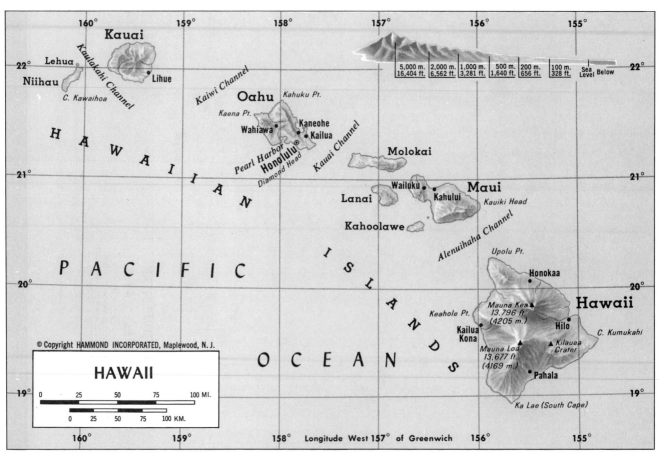

Kauai

Lehua

Niihau

Kaulakahi Channel

C. Kawaihoa

Lihue

Kaiwi Channel

| 5,000 m. 16,404 ft. | 2,000 m. 6,562 ft. | 1,000 m. 3,281 ft. | 500 m. 1,640 ft. | 200 m. 656 ft. | 100 m. 328 ft. | Sea Level Below |

Oahu

Kahuku Pt.

Kaena Pt.

Wahiawa

• Kaneohe
• Kailua

H

Pearl Harbor

Honolulu

Diamond Head

Kauai Channel

Molokai

A

W

A

I

I

A

N

Lanai

Wailuku

Kahului

Maui

Kauiki Head

Kahoolawe

Alenuihaha Channel

PACIFIC

I

S

L

A

N

D

S

Upolu Pt.

• Honokaa

Keahole Pt.

Mauna Kea ▲
13,796 ft.
(4205 m.)

Hawaii

• Hilo

Kailua
Kona

Kilauea
Crater

C. Kumukahi

© Copyright HAMMOND INCORPORATED, Maplewood, N.J.

OCEAN

Mauna Loa
13,677 ft.
(4169 m.)

• Pahala

HAWAII

0 25 50 75 100 MI.

0 25 50 75 100 KM.

Ka Lae (South Cape)

Longitude West 157° of Greenwich

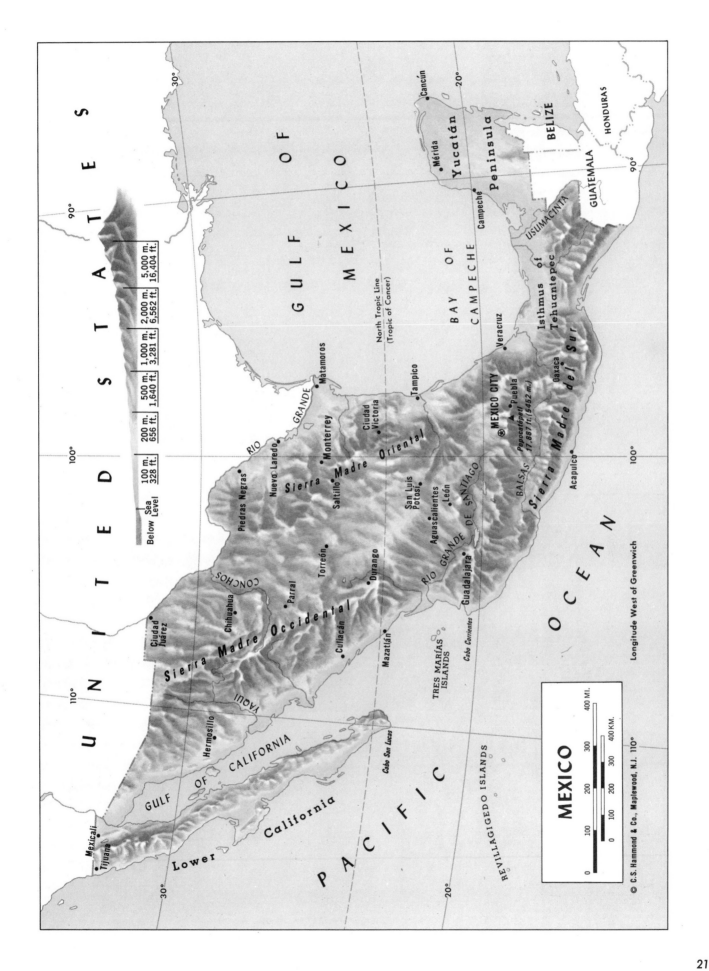

MEXICO

100 m. 200 m. 500 m. 1,000 m. 2,000 m. 5,000 m.
328 ft. 656 ft. 1,640 ft. 3,281 ft. 6,562 ft. 16,404 ft.

Sea
Level

Below
Sea
Level

UNITED STATES

GULF OF MEXICO

BAY OF CAMPECHE

Yucatán Peninsula

BELIZE

HONDURAS

GUATEMALA

Cancún

Mérida

Campeche

USUMACINTA

Isthmus of Tehuantepec

Sierra Madre del Sur

Oaxaca

Veracruz

Puebla

Popocatépetl
17,887 ft. (5452 m.)

⊗ MEXICO CITY

Acapulco

BALSAS

Guadalajara

RIO GRANDE DE SANTIAGO

León

Aguascalientes

San Luis Potosí

Saltillo

Ciudad Victoria

Sierra Madre Oriental

Monterrey

Nuevo Laredo

Matamoros

Tampico

North Tropic Line
(Tropic of Cancer)

Piedras Negras

RIO GRANDE

Chihuahua

Ciudad Juárez

Parral

Torreón

Durango

CONCHOS

Sierra Madre Occidental

Culiacán

Mazatlán

TRES MARÍAS
ISLANDS

Cabo Corrientes

YAQUI

Hermosillo

CALIFORNIA

GULF OF CALIFORNIA

Cabo San Lucas

Lower California

Mexicali

Tijuana

PACIFIC OCEAN

REVILLAGIGEDO ISLANDS

Longitude West of Greenwich

MEXICO

400 MI.

0   100   200   300

0   100   200   300   400 KM.

© C.S. Hammond & Co., Maplewood, N.J. 110°

30°

90°

100°

110°

20°

90°

100°

30°

20°

21

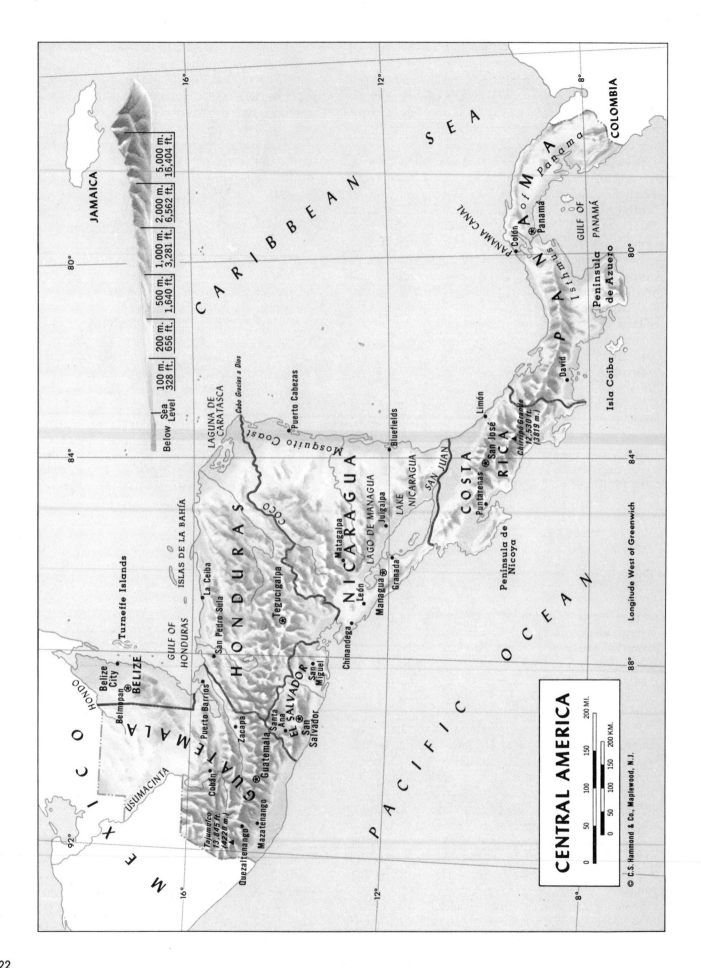

CENTRAL AMERICA

JAMAICA

CARIBBEAN SEA

	100 m.	200 m.	500 m.	1,000 m.	2,000 m.	5,000 m.
Below Sea Level	328 ft.	656 ft.	1,640 ft.	3,281 ft.	6,562 ft.	16,404 ft.

COLOMBIA

C E N T R A L   A M E R I C A

Panama
Panamá
Colón
PANAMA CANAL
Isthmus of Panama
GULF OF PANAMÁ
Peninsula de Azuero
David
Isla Coiba
80°
8°

Limón
San José
COSTA RICA
Chirripó Grande
12,530 ft.
(3819 m.)
Puntarenas
Peninsula de Nicoya
84°

Bluefields
SAN JUAN
LAKE NICARAGUA
LAGO DE MANAGUA
Juigalpa
Granada
Managua
León
NICARAGUA
Matagalpa
Chinandega

Puerto Cabezas
Cabo Gracias a Dios
LAGUNA DE CARATASCA
Mosquito Coast
COCO
88°

La Ceiba
San Pedro Sula
H O N D U R A S
Tegucigalpa
ISLAS DE LA BAHÍA
GULF OF HONDURAS
Turneffe Islands

BELIZE
Belize City
Belmopan
HONDO
Puerto Barrios
Zacapa
Cobán
Guatemala
G U A T E M A L A
Mazatenango
Quezaltenango
Tajumulco
13,845 ft.
(4220 m.)
USUMACINTA

Santa Ana
San Salvador
EL SALVADOR
San Miguel

M E X I C O
92°
16°
12°

P A C I F I C   O C E A N

Longitude West of Greenwich
84°
88°
8°
12°

CENTRAL AMERICA

0	50	100	150	200 MI.
0	50	100	150	200 KM.

© C.S. Hammond & Co., Maplewood, N.J.

CENTRAL AMERICA

Connecting the North American and South American continents is a long, narrow stretch of land called an isthmus. This area is often called Central America even though it is the southernmost part of North America. The seven independent nations that form Central America are bounded on the west by the Pacific Ocean and on the east by the Caribbean Sea.

Because almost all of Central America lies between the equator and 18° north latitude, the climate is relatively hot, and rainfall frequent. The highest point in Central America, Tajumulco, Guatemala, is 13,845 feet above sea level. Many of the mountains that form Central America are active volcanos.

The sunshine and rainfall, combined with the fertile Central American soil, support thriving farming and livestock industries. Coffee, sugarcane, bananas, cotton, rice, and livestock, the chief Central American agricultural products, are the major exports.

Since prehistoric times, the isthmus has served as a passageway for animals, and later people migrating first to South America and, then, back and forth between the continents.

Indians were among the early inhabitants of Central America. In the 1500s, however, the Spanish conquered the Indians. Today, the population of Central America is a mixture of people of Indian, European, Asian, and African descent.

In 1903, the United States and Panama established a treaty which gave the United States the right to build a canal through Panama. Find the Panama Canal on your map. The United States was given exclusive control of the canal, and in 1914 it was opened. However, for many years Panamanians have wanted to amend the treaty and limit American control over the waterway. In 1977, under the Carter Administration, the United States and Panama signed a new treaty. The treaty provides for transfer of the canal to Panama by the year 2000.

1. Look at the map of the world on page 4. Why does it make sense to build a canal through Central America? What would be the effect on worldwide shipping were the canal not there?
2. Find El Salvador on the map. The pressure of overpopulation has led to constant political unrest within this nation. In addition, the dense population has led its neighbors to fear that El Salvador might attempt to expand into their territories. Research the history of this country from 1969, and try to find other reasons for the political unrest. What role has the United States played in the recent history of this country? Why are Americans divided about the role of the United States in El Salvador? This information is readily available in newspapers and magazines.

THE WEST INDIES   MAP—PAGE 24

East of Central America and Mexico lie the West Indies. This group of islands has two major divisions: the Greater Antilles and the Lesser Antilles. The Greater Antilles, the larger group of islands, includes Cuba, Jamaica, Hispaniola (Haiti and the Dominican Republic share the island), and Puerto Rico. The islands of the Lesser Antilles extend southerly from Puerto Rico to Trinidad and west to Aruba.

The climate in the West Indies is warm all year around. Ample rainfall and cool breezes offset the very warm temperatures during June, July, and August.

The West Indies are formed by mountains whose peaks reach above the sea. The highest point is Pico Duarte in the Dominican Republic (10,417 feet). Some of the islands in the Lesser Antilles are active volcanos.

Because most of the islands lack mineral resources, except for limited minerals in Trinidad, Cuba, and Jamaica, the economy of the islands depends heavily on farming. Tropical fruits, coffee, sugar, and spices are among the farm products. Sugar cane is the leading product.

Some of the islands have advanced economically through limited industrialization. Puerto Rico was one of the first islands to successfully develop industry.

Tourism has also stimulated the economy of the West Indies. Over the past 20 years, income from both tourism and industry has led to a higher standard of living on the islands. Some of the islands, however, are still poverty-ridden because of overpopulation. On several islands, civil strife and political instability have also hindered economic growth.

When Columbus discovered the West Indies, Indians occupied the islands. Then, as more Europeans began migrating to the islands, the Indian population declined. Europeans also brought slaves from Africa. Many descendants of these slaves have remained on the islands. Today, on most of the islands, the population is composed of many different ethnic groups.

1. The history of the Dominican Republic is plagued by violence and bloodshed. Research the history of this country. Then study the Dominican Republic today. How has the unrest in this country affected its growth? If you had to speculate on the future of the Dominican Republic, what conclusions would you draw, based upon its past? What improvements do you see? What problems do you see?

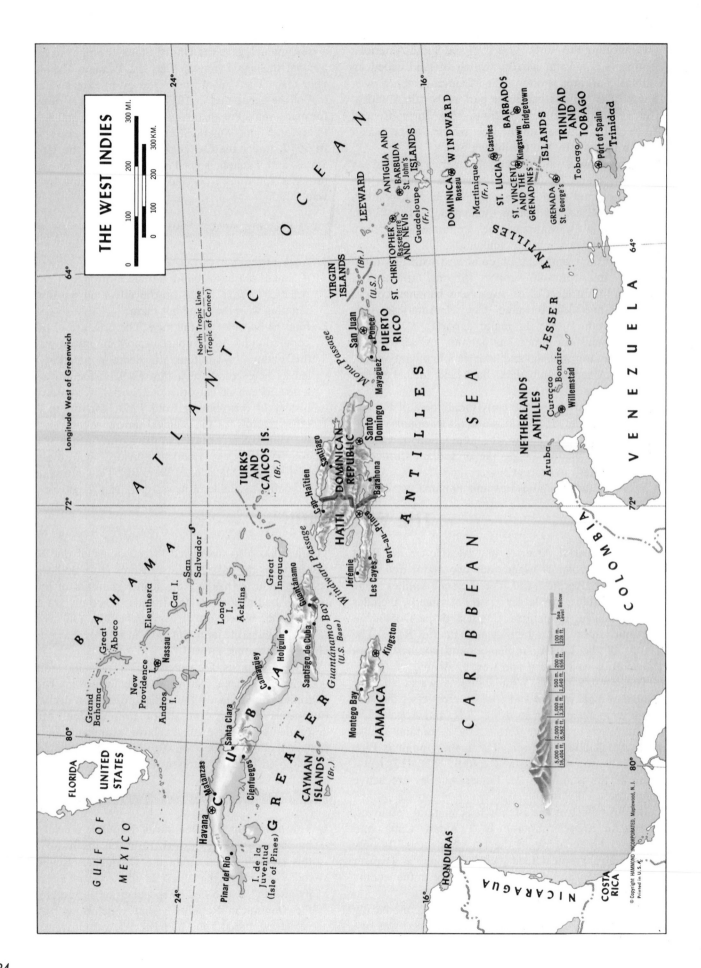

THE WEST INDIES

300 MI.

0 100 200 300 K.M.

FLORIDA

UNITED STATES

GULF OF MEXICO

Grand Bahama

Great Abaco

New Providence I.

Nassau

Andros I.

Eleuthera I.

Cat I.

San Salvador

B A H A M A S

Long I.

Acklins I.

Great Inagua

Havana
Matanzas
Santa Clara
Cienfuegos
Pinar del Río
I. de la Juventud (Isle of Pines)

C U B A

Camagüey
Holguín
Santiago de Cuba
Guantánamo
Guantánamo Bay (U.S. Base)

G R E A T E R

CAYMAN ISLANDS (Br.)

Montego Bay

JAMAICA

Kingston

Windward Passage

Jérémie
Les Cayes
Port-au-Prince
Cap-Haïtien
Gonaïves
Santiago
Barahona

HAITI

DOMINICAN REPUBLIC

Santo Domingo

TURKS AND CAICOS IS. (Br.)

North Tropic Line (Tropic of Cancer)

Longitude West of Greenwich

A T L A N T I C O C E A N

Mona Passage

Mayagüez
San Juan
Ponce

PUERTO RICO

VIRGIN ISLANDS (Br.)
(U.S.)

LEEWARD

ST. CHRISTOPHER AND NEVIS
Basseterre

ANTIGUA AND BARBUDA
St. John's

Guadeloupe (Fr.)

ISLANDS

DOMINICA
Roseau

Martinique (Fr.)

WINDWARD

ST. LUCIA
Castries

BARBADOS
Bridgetown

ST. VINCENT AND THE GRENADINES
Kingstown

ISLANDS

GRENADA
St. George's

TRINIDAD AND TOBAGO
Tobago
Port of Spain
Trinidad

A N T I L L E S

L E S S E R

A N T I L L E S

C A R I B B E A N   S E A

NETHERLANDS ANTILLES

Aruba
Curaçao
Bonaire
Willemstad

V E N E Z U E L A

C O L O M B I A

HONDURAS

NICARAGUA

COSTA RICA

5,000 m. 16,404 ft. | 2,000 m. 6,562 ft. | 1,000 m. 3,281 ft. | 500 m. 1,640 ft. | 200 m. 656 ft. | 100 m. 328 ft. | Sea Level | Below

© Copyright HAMMOND INCORPORATED, Maplewood, N.J.
Printed in U.S.A.

24

SOUTH AMERICA

South America is the fourth largest continent and the southernmost of the two continents in the Western Hemisphere. It is connected to North America at the Isthmus of Panama. Most of South America lies south of the equator, and it extends southwards to about 600 miles (970 kilometers) from the continent of Antarctica.

The coastline of South America is fairly regular. It has no large bays, gulfs, or large peninsulas as do some of the other continents. A chain of rugged islands lies off southwestern Chile. In the extreme south, Tierra del Fuego is separated from the mainland by the Strait of Magellan. Other islands are the Falklands off southeastern Argentina and the Galapagos off Ecuador.

If you look at the map, you will notice that South America has two outstanding features—a series of high mountains running along the west coast and a great river stretching across the continent. A closer study will show you that the geographical features of South America are similar to those of North America in some ways. As North America, South America has highlands on the east coast and inland plains. But the two continents are not very much alike in climate and vegetation.

With the equator crossing South America near its broadest width, most of the continent lies in the tropics. In the lowland area of the Amazon it is hot and humid the year round. Temperatures get progressively cooler at higher elevations. But in South America, even at higher elevations, the temperatures are not very low. In fact, in the plateau areas of the mountains, thousands of feet above sea level, the Indians and Spaniards established large settlements. The temperatures to the south of the equator are more moderate. But even at the southernmost tip, the weather does not become extremely cold.

Rainfall varies from very heavy, exceeding 100 inches (254 centimeters) annually in parts of the rainforests, to very light along the west coast between northern Chile and northern Peru. The Atacama Desert here is one of the driest areas on earth. Rainfall has never been recorded in some places of this desert.

The Andes are part of the great cordillera, or line of mountains, that extends the entire length of North America. In South America they rise steeply from the Pacific in long ranges of snow-capped peaks and wide plateaus. In the north, the Andes spread out into three separate branches. Farther south, the Andes widen to as much as 400 miles (644 kilometers) in Bolivia and enclose a series of high and wide flat areas called the *Altiplano,* or the Bolivian Plateau. To the south the range narrows and lowers to form a single range. It extends off the southern coast of Chile in a ragged fringe of islands. Mt. Aconcagua in west-central Argentina near the Chilean border is the highest point in the Western Hemisphere. The Andes contain many volcanoes, many of which are still active.

In the eastern part of South America there are two areas of highlands that might be compared to the Appalachians of North America. In the north are the mostly unexplored Guiana Highlands. The Brazilian Highlands are in the east-central South America. Both highland regions have rounded hills and worn-down mountains. Around their edges are steep cliffs over which rivers fall and rush to the sea. These rough waters hinder transportation on the rivers but they are possible sources of water power. The Brazilian Highlands are rich in minerals, and the soil is fertile. It is one of South America's important farming, grazing, and industrial areas.

In southern Argentina the cold, windy, dry tableland of Patagonia resembles the Laurentian Plateau of Canada. It is used mainly to graze sheep.

There are grassy plains, or *Llanos,* in the north near the Orinoco River. In Paraguay and northern Argentina, is the *Gran Chaco,* an area of low bushes and trees and grasslands. The most fertile of South America's plains is the *Pampas* of Argentina, a luxuriant grassland and one of the world's great agricultural regions. The plains of South America are more walled in with mountains and highlands than those of North America. That makes them more difficult to reach.

The lowlands are crossed by rivers. The largest lowland area is drained by the Amazon, the second-largest river in the world, after the Nile. With its tributaries, it forms the largest river system in the world. The Amazon drains over one-third of the continent and carries more water than any other river. It is navigable for 2,300 miles (3,700 kilometers) from the Atlantic Ocean to Iquitos in Peru. There are very few major cities along the river. Off the Amazon, transportation is extremely difficult because the area is covered with *selvas*—dense rainforests. The Brazilian government is building a highway through Amazonas and bringing in settlers to develop the region.

Other important rivers of South America are the Río de la Plata, the São Francisco, and the Orinoco.

---

1. List the four main lowland areas of South America.
2. Why is the Amazon River called the largest river system in the world?
3. One country has two capital cities. What is the country? What are its capitals?

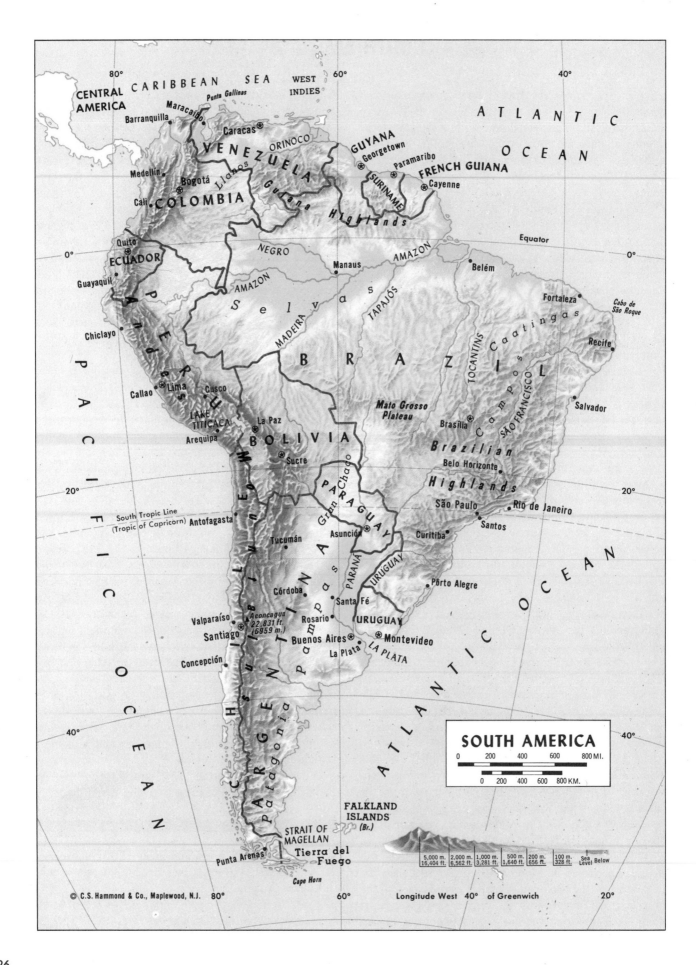

CENTRAL AMERICA

CARIBBEAN SEA

WEST INDIES

ATLANTIC OCEAN

80° 60° 40°

Punta Gallinas
Maracaibo
Barranquilla
Caracas ⊛
VENEZUELA
ORINOCO
GUYANA
Georgetown ⊛
Paramaribo
SURINAME
FRENCH GUIANA
Cayenne ⊛

Medellín
Bogotá ⊛
Cali
COLOMBIA
Llanos
Guiana
Highlands

Quito ⊛
ECUADOR
NEGRO
Manaus
AMAZON
Equator
Belém
0° 0°

Guayaquil
AMAZON
Selvas
TAPAJÓS
Fortaleza
Cabo de São Roque

Chiclayo
ANDES
MADEIRA
BRAZIL
Caatingas
Recife

PERU
TOCANTINS
Campos
SÃO FRANCISCO

Callao
Lima
Cusco
Mato Grosso Plateau
Salvador

LAKE TITICACA
La Paz
Brasília ⊛
Brazilian

Arequipa
BOLIVIA
Belo Horizonte
Highlands

Sucre ⊛
Chaco
20° 20°

South Tropic Line (Tropic of Capricorn)
Antofagasta
PARAGUAY
Gran
São Paulo
Rio de Janeiro

Tucumán
Asunción ⊛
Santos

ARGENTINA
PARANÁ
Curitiba
URUGUAY

Córdoba
Santa Fé
Pôrto Alegre

Valparaíso
Aconcagua 22,831 ft. (6959 m.)
Rosario
URUGUAY

Santiago
Buenos Aires ⊛
Montevideo ⊛

Pampas
La Plata
LA PLATA

Concepción
CHILE

PACIFIC OCEAN

Patagonia

40° 40°

ATLANTIC OCEAN

FALKLAND ISLANDS (Br.)

STRAIT OF MAGELLAN
Punta Arenas
Tierra del Fuego

Cape Horn

© C.S. Hammond & Co., Maplewood, N.J.   80°   60°   Longitude West   40°   of Greenwich   20°

SOUTH AMERICA

0   200   400   600   800 MI.

0   200   400   600   800 KM.

| 5,000 m. 16,404 ft. | 2,000 m. 6,562 ft. | 1,000 m. 3,281 ft. | 500 m. 1,640 ft. | 200 m. 656 ft. | 100 m. 328 ft. | Sea Level | Below |

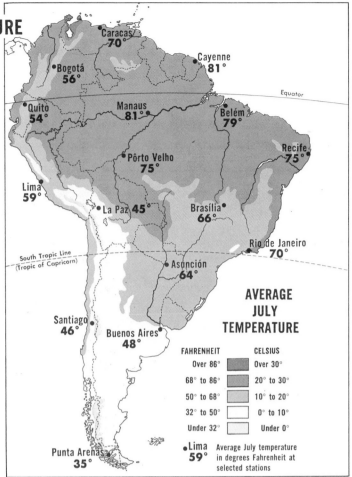

TEMPERATURE

AVERAGE JANUARY TEMPERATURE

Caracas 64°
Bogotá 57°
Cayenne 81°
Quito 54°
Manaus 79°
Belém 77°
Pôrto Velho 77°
Recife 81°
Lima 72°
La Paz 52°
Brasília 70°
Asunción 83°
Rio de Janeiro 79°
Santiago 66°
Buenos Aires 75°
Punta Arenas 48°

Equator

South Tropic Line (Tropic of Capricorn)

FAHRENHEIT		CELSIUS
Over 86°		Over 30°
68° to 86°		20° to 30°
50° to 68°		10° to 20°
32° to 50°		0° to 10°
		Under 0°

• Lima 72° Average January temperature in degrees Fahrenheit at selected stations

AVERAGE JULY TEMPERATURE

Caracas 70°
Bogotá 56°
Cayenne 81°
Quito 54°
Manaus 81°
Belém 79°
Pôrto Velho 75°
Recife 75°
Lima 59°
La Paz 45°
Brasília 66°
Asunción 64°
Rio de Janeiro 70°
Santiago 46°
Buenos Aires 48°
Punta Arenas 35°

Equator

South Tropic Line (Tropic of Capricorn)

FAHRENHEIT		CELSIUS
Over 86°		Over 30°
68° to 86°		20° to 30°
50° to 68°		10° to 20°
32° to 50°		0° to 10°
Under 32°		Under 0°

• Lima 59° Average July temperature in degrees Fahrenheit at selected stations

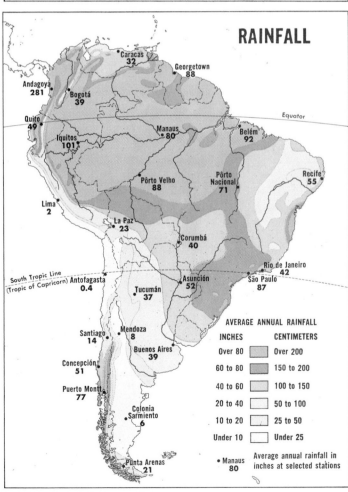

RAINFALL

Caracas 32
Georgetown 88
Andagoya 281
Bogotá 39
Quito 49
Iquitos 101
Manaus 80
Belém 92
Pôrto Velho 88
Pôrto Nacional 71
Recife 55
Lima 2
La Paz 23
Corumbá 40
Rio de Janeiro 42
Antofagasta 0.4
Tucumán 37
Asunción 52
São Paulo 87
Santiago 14
Mendoza 8
Buenos Aires 39
Concepción 51
Puerto Montt 77
Colonia Sarmiento 6
Punta Arenas 21

Equator

South Tropic Line (Tropic of Capricorn)

AVERAGE ANNUAL RAINFALL

INCHES		CENTIMETERS
Over 80		Over 200
60 to 80		150 to 200
40 to 60		100 to 150
20 to 40		50 to 100
10 to 20		25 to 50
Under 10		Under 25

• Manaus 80 Average annual rainfall in inches at selected stations

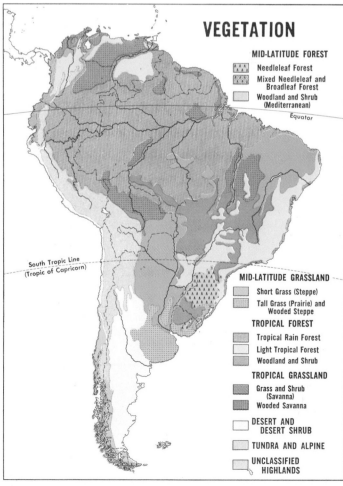

VEGETATION

Equator

South Tropic Line (Tropic of Capricorn)

MID-LATITUDE FOREST
- Needleleaf Forest
- Mixed Needleleaf and Broadleaf Forest
- Woodland and Shrub (Mediterranean)

MID-LATITUDE GRASSLAND
- Short Grass (Steppe)
- Tall Grass (Prairie) and Wooded Steppe

TROPICAL FOREST
- Tropical Rain Forest
- Light Tropical Forest
- Woodland and Shrub

TROPICAL GRASSLAND
- Grass and Shrub (Savanna)
- Wooded Savanna

DESERT AND DESERT SHRUB

TUNDRA AND ALPINE

UNCLASSIFIED HIGHLANDS

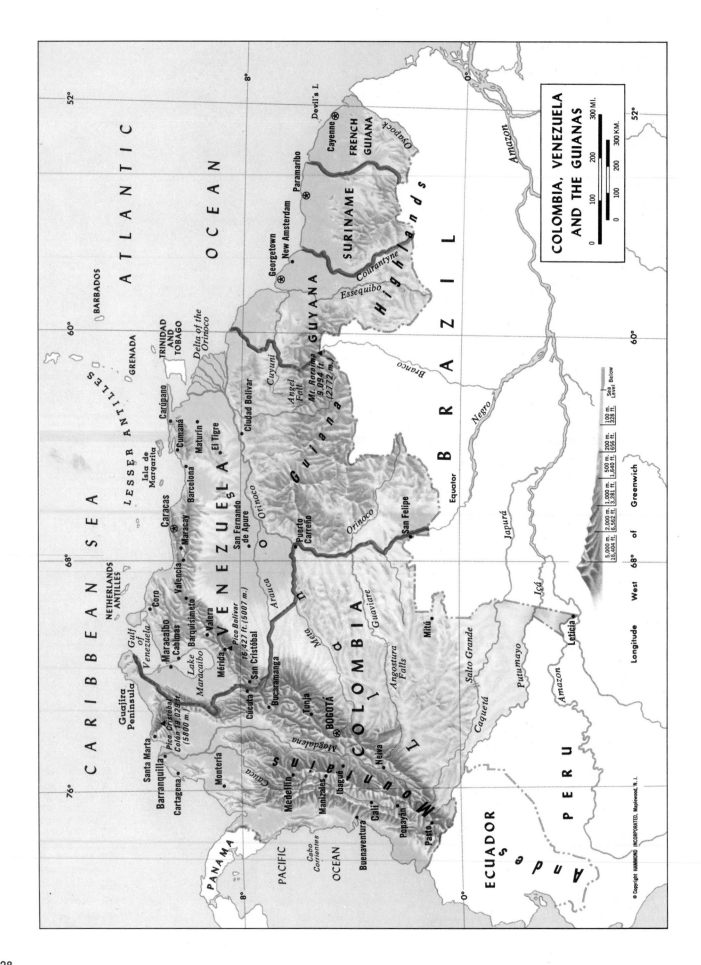

COLOMBIA, VENEZUELA
AND THE GUIANAS

300 MI.
300 KM.

CARIBBEAN SEA

ATLANTIC OCEAN

BARBADOS

LESSER ANTILLES

GRENADA

TRINIDAD AND TOBAGO

Delta of the Orinoco

NETHERLANDS ANTILLES

Isla de Margarita

Carúpano
Cumaná
Maturín
Barcelona
El Tigre
Caracas
Maracay
San Fernando de Apure
Valencia
Coro
Barquisimeto
Valera
Maracaibo
Cabimas

VENEZUELA

Guajira Peninsula

Gulf of Venezuela

Lake Maracaibo

Pico Bolívar
16,427 ft. (5007 m.)

Mérida
San Cristóbal

Santa Marta
Barranquilla
Cartagena

Pico Cristóbal
Colón 19,029 ft.
(5800 m.)

Montería

Medellín
Manizales
Ibagué
Buenaventura
Cali
Popayán
Pasto

Cabo Corrientes

PACIFIC OCEAN

PANAMA

Cauca

COLOMBIA

Mountains

Andes

Bucaramanga
Tunja
BOGOTÁ
Neiva

Magdalena

Cúcuta

Arauca

Meta

Guaviare

Angostura Falls

Mitú

Salto Grande

Caquetá

Putumayo

Icá

Amazon

Leticia

Japurá

ECUADOR

PERU

Ciudad Bolívar
Puerto Carreño
San Felipe

Orinoco

Orinoco

Cuyuni

Angel Fall

Mt. Roraima
9,094 ft.
(2772 m.)

Guiana Highlands

BRAZIL

Branco

Negro

Amazon

Georgetown
New Amsterdam
Paramaribo

GUYANA

SURINAME

FRENCH GUIANA

Cayenne

Devil's I.

Essequibo
Courantyne
Oyapock

Equator

52°
60°
68°
76°

8°
0°
8°

0°

Longitude   West   68°   of   Greenwich

5,000 m.
16,404 ft.
2,000 m.
6,562 ft.
1,000 m.
3,281 ft.
500 m.
1,640 ft.
200 m.
656 ft.
100 m.
328 ft.
Sea Level
Below

© Copyright HAMMOND INCORPORATED, Maplewood, N.J.

28

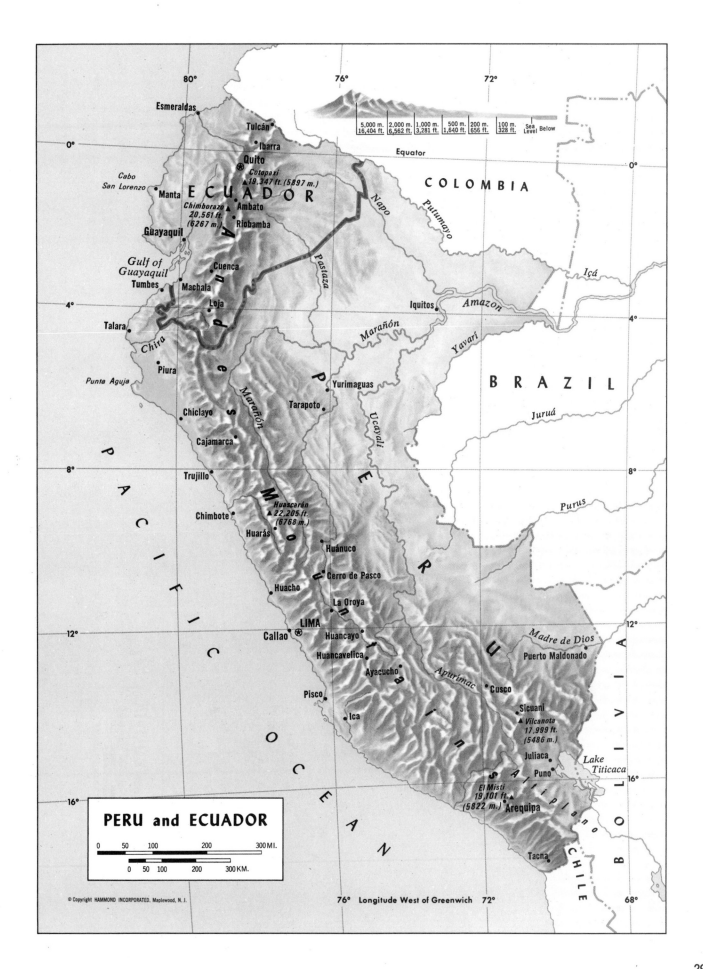

Esmeraldas

80°

76°

72°

5,000 m. | 2,000 m. | 1,000 m. | 500 m. | 200 m. | 100 m. | Sea | Below
16,404 ft. | 6,562 ft. | 3,281 ft. | 1,640 ft. | 656 ft. | 328 ft. | Level

Tulcán

Equator

0°

0°

COLOMBIA

Ibarra

Quito

Cotopaxi
▲ *19,347 ft. (5897 m.)*

*Cabo
San Lorenzo*

E C U A D O R

Napo

Putumayo

Içá

Manta

Chimborazo ▲ Ambato
20,561 ft.
(6267 m.)   Riobamba

A

Guayaquil

Pastaza

*Gulf of
Guayaquil*

n

Cuenca

Tumbes

Machala

d

Marañón

Loja

Iquitos

Amazon

4°

4°

Talara

Chira

e

P

Yavari

Piura

s

B R A Z I L

Punta Aguja

Chiclayo

Marañón

Yurimaguas

Juruá

E

Tarapoto

Cajamarca

Ucayali

8°

8°

Trujillo

M

R

Purus

Huascarán
▲ *22,205 ft.
(6768 m.)*

Chimbote

Huarás

o

Huánuco

U

Cerro de Pasco

u

Huacho

La Oroya

Madre de Dios

12°

Puerto Maldonado

12°

LIMA

n

Huancayo

Callao

U

Huancavelica

Apurímac

t

Ayacucho

Cusco

a

Pisco

Sicuani
▲ *Vilcanota
17,999 ft.
(5486 m.)*

Ica

i

Juliaca

n

*Lake
Titicaca*

Puno

s

*El Misti
19,101 ft. ▲
(5822 m.)* Arequipa

altiplano

16°

16°

B

O

L

I

V

I

A

P

A

C

I

F

I

C

Tacna

C

H

I

L

E

O

C

E

A

N

PERU and ECUADOR

0   50   100   200   300 MI.

0   50 100   200   300 KM.

76°   Longitude West of Greenwich   72°

68°

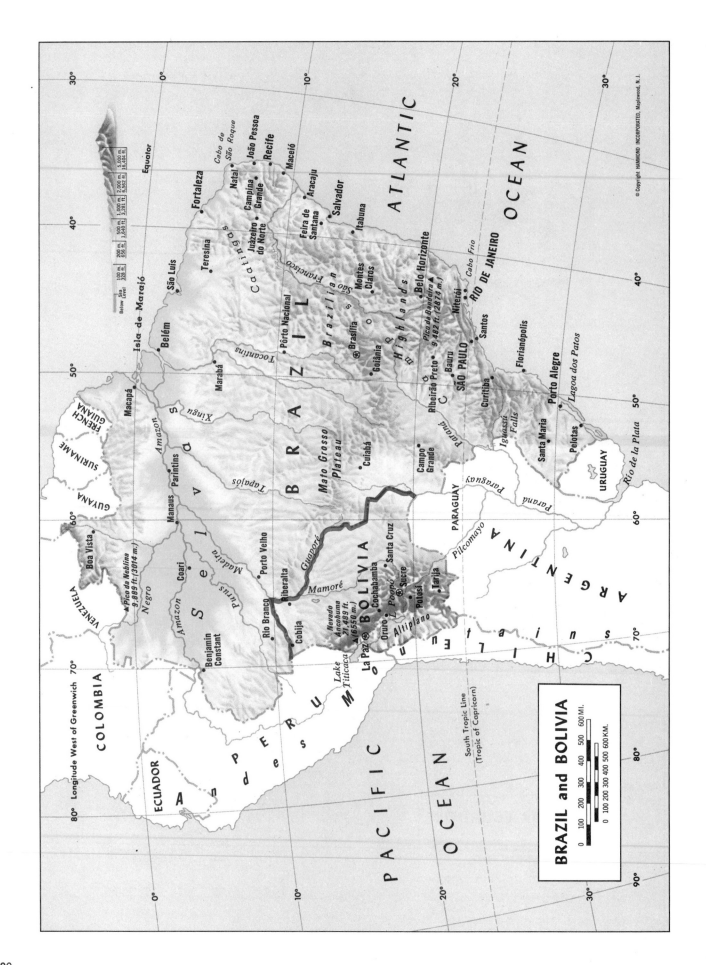

Below Sea Level | 100 m. 328 ft. | 200 m. 656 ft. | 500 m. 1,640 ft. | 1,000 m. 3,281 ft. | 2,000 m. 6,562 ft. | 5,000 m. 16,404 ft.

© Copyright HAMMOND INCORPORATED, Maplewood, N.J.

ATLANTIC OCEAN

PACIFIC OCEAN

BRAZIL and BOLIVIA

600 MI.
0 100 200 300 400 500

600 KM.
0 100 200 300 400 500

COLOMBIA
ECUADOR
PERU
VENEZUELA
FRENCH GUIANA
SURINAME
GUYANA
BOLIVIA
PARAGUAY
ARGENTINA
CHILE
URUGUAY

BRAZIL

Andes
Selvas
Mato Grosso Plateau
Brazilian Highlands
Caatingas
Cordilleras

Equator
Longitude West of Greenwich
South Tropic Line
(Tropic of Capricorn)

Cabo de São Roque
João Pessoa
Recife
Maceió
Natal
Campina Grande
Aracaju
Salvador
Itabuna
Fortaleza
Feira de Santana
Teresina
Juazeiro do Norte
São Luís
Belém
Macapá
Marabá
Pôrto Nacional
Brasília
Goiânia
Montes Claros
Belo Horizonte
Pico da Bandeira ▲ 9,482 ft. (2,873 m.)
Niterói
Cabo Frio
RIO DE JANEIRO
Santos
SÃO PAULO
Ribeirão Prêto
Bauru
Curitiba
Florianópolis
Pôrto Alegre
Santa Maria
Pelotas
Iguassú Falls
Lagoa dos Patos
Rio de la Plata
Cuiabá
Campo Grande
Boa Vista
Manaus
Parintins
Coari
Benjamin Constant
Pôrto Velho
Rio Branco
Cobija
Riberalta
Santa Cruz
Cochabamba
Sucre
Potosí
Tarija
Oruro
La Paz
Lake Titicaca
Nevado Ancohuma 21,489 ft. (6,550 m.)
Altiplano
L. Poopó
Pico da Neblina 9,889 ft. (3,014 m.)

Amazon
Negro
Madeira
Purus
Tapajós
Xingu
Tocantins
São Francisco
Guaporé
Mamoré
Paraná
Paraguay
Pilcomayo
Isla de Marajó

30

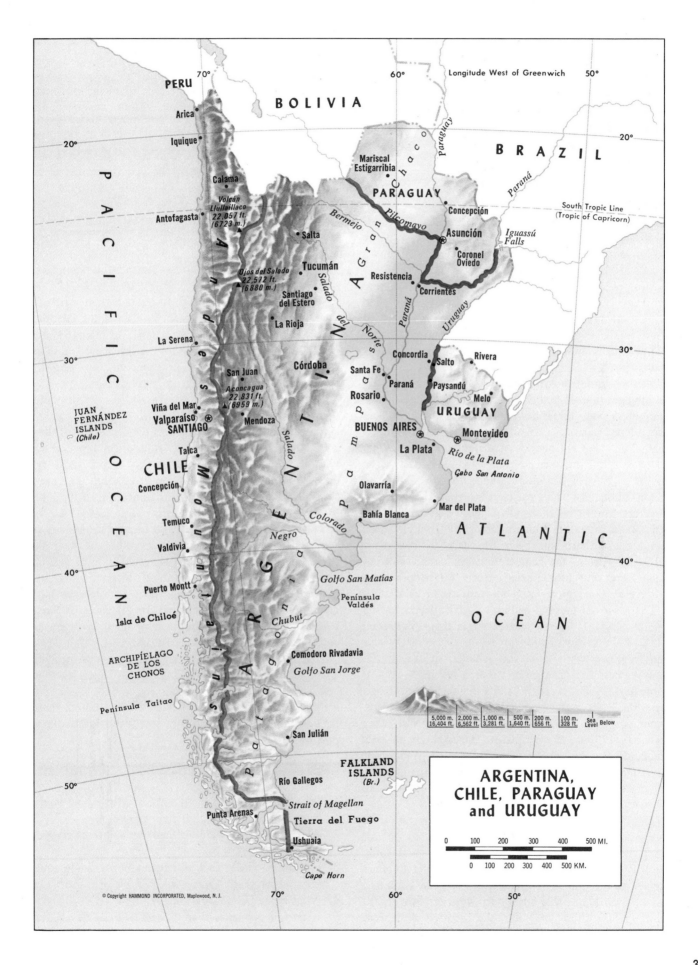

PERU

BOLIVIA

Arica

Iquique

PACIFIC

Calama

*Volcán
Llullaillaco
22,057 ft.
(6723 m.)*

Antofagasta

Salta

Longitude West of Greenwich

BRAZIL

Mariscal
Estigarribia

Chaco

Paraguay

PARAGUAY

Concepción

Pilcomayo

Asunción

Coronel
Oviedo

Paraná

South Tropic Line
(Tropic of Capricorn)

*Iguassú
Falls*

O
C
E
A
N

Tucumán

*Ojos del Salado
22,572 ft.
(6880 m.)*

Santiago
del Estero

La Rioja

La Serena

San Juan

*Aconcagua
22,831 ft.
(6959 m.)*

Córdoba

Viña del Mar
Valparaíso
SANTIAGO

Mendoza

JUAN
FERNÁNDEZ
ISLANDS
(Chile)

Talca

CHILE

Concepción

Temuco

Valdivia

Puerto Montt

Isla de Chiloé

ARCHIPÍELAGO
DE LOS
CHONOS

Península Taitao

Bermejo

Gran

Salado

del

Norte

Resistencia

Corrientes

Paraná

Uruguay

Concordia

Santa Fe

Paraná

Rosario

Pampa

BUENOS AIRES

La Plata

Salto

Paysandú

Rivera

Melo

URUGUAY

Montevideo

Río de la Plata

Cabo San Antonio

Olavarría

Colorado

Bahía Blanca

Mar del Plata

ATLANTIC

Negro

Golfo San Matías

Península
Valdés

OCEAN

Chubut

Salado

A
R
G
E
N
T
I
N
A

A
n
d
e
s

M
o
u
n
t
a
i
n
s

Patagonia

Comodoro Rivadavia

Golfo San Jorge

San Julián

FALKLAND
ISLANDS
(Br.)

Río Gallegos

Strait of Magellan

Punta Arenas

Tierra del Fuego

Ushuaia

Cape Horn

5,000 m.
16,404 ft. | 2,000 m.
6,562 ft. | 1,000 m.
3,281 ft. | 500 m.
1,640 ft. | 200 m.
656 ft. | 100 m.
328 ft. | Sea
Level | Below

ARGENTINA,
CHILE, PARAGUAY
and URUGUAY

0   100   200   300   400   500 MI.

0   100   200   300   400   500 KM.

70°   60°   50°

AFRICA

Africa, the second largest continent, is cut almost in half by the equator. Because the bulge of land in western Africa is so large, most of Africa lies in the Northern Hemisphere.

For the most part, Africa has a smooth coastline. There are no large bays or deep inlets to form natural harbors. The majority of Africa's seaports are in the north along the Mediterranean Sea.

Africa does not have a great many islands lying off its coasts. Madagascar, the fourth largest island in the world, is off the southeast coast. Many of Africa's islands are independent countries.

Most of Africa is a high plateau. Its height ranges between 2,000 feet (610 meters) and 5,000 feet (1,524 meters) above sea level. This tableland is lower in the north and west and higher in the south and east. It is almost surrounded by a narrow, coastal plain.

Various parts of Africa have different climates, depending on rainfall and elevation. In North Africa, for example, where there is very little rain, the plateau has a desert climate. Around the equator the rainfall is heavy and there are periods of torrential rain. The low plateaus in this area are covered with dense rainforests, and it is always hot and humid. In the equatorial regions in the east where the land is higher, the temperatures are lower and there are extensive grasslands. In general, the climate is cooler in areas of higher elevation and in the northern and southern parts of the continent. In South Africa, the temperate climate and lack of dense rainforests have made it easier for people there to develop the region's rich mineral resources.

The most outstanding feature of Africa by far is the Sahara desert. It covers an area larger than the United States and stretches southward from the Atlas Mountains and westward from the Atlantic Ocean to the Red Sea across a distance of about 3,200 miles (5,150 kilometers). The Sahara is a dry region that supports little life. Some parts have shifting sand dunes (*ergs*). Other parts are covered with pebbles. And still other sections are bare rocky plains. Among the desert's highlands are the Ahaggar of Algeria, the Tibesti of Chad and Libya, and the Aïr of Niger. In the east the Sahara is made up of a number of smaller deserts—the Libyan, Arabian, and Nubian deserts.

The desert has a number of shallow streams and rivers during periods of rainfall. These rivers do not reach the coast and usually peter out in the sand. Only the Nile carries a large enough volume of water to reach the sea all the time. From its sources in Lake Tana and Lake Victoria, the Nile flows northward for over 4,100 miles (6,600 kilometers) into the Mediterranean Sea.

With its seasonal flooding, the Nile turns the surrounding land into a fertile valley. Oases can be found scattered throughout the Sahara. Their water comes from springs and wells. Other deserts of Africa are the Kalahari and the Great Karoo in the south. The Sahara is the dividing line between the Arab nations to the north and the mainly Black nations to the south.

In the northwest corner of the continent and paralleling the coast are the rugged Atlas Mountains. They are a continuation of the Alpine system of southern Europe, and they have some plateau regions within them. These mountains separate the northwest coastal plain from the Sahara.

The main mountain range in southeastern Africa is the Drakensberg. It lies between Swaziland and Lesotho. North of the Drakensberg are a series of highlands and plateaus that extend northward to the Red Sea. This region is the highest part of the continent, and the Ethiopian Highlands form its highest section.

Running through these eastern highlands from Ethiopia southwards to Mozambique is a long depression, or opening in the earth, known as the Great Rift Valley. Actually it begins in Syria and runs under the Red Sea to northeastern Ethiopia. Long ago, huge cracks occurred in the earth, and the land in between the cracks sank to form a series of valleys. Almost all of the lakes in east Africa are part of the rift. Only Lake Victoria, Africa's largest lake, is not. The highest mountains of Africa are towering volcanic peaks that lie near the rift valleys. They include Mt. Kilimanjaro in Tanzania, which is the highest mountain in Africa, and Mt. Kenya in Kenya. The lava from volcanoes in this area have given much of it very fertile soil. In the past, the Great Rift Valley prevented the development of extensive communication between the east and west.

Africa has a number of long rivers besides the Nile. They include the Congo (Zaire), the Niger, Orange, and Zambezi. Many of Africa's rivers have rapids and waterfalls, which are obstacles to transportation. Some have sandbars at the mouth or low water levels during part of the year.

---

1. Two countries have capital cities on the Nile River. Name the countries and their capitals.
2. What important waterway links the Mediterranean Sea with the Red Sea?
3. List the countries that lie entirely between the equator and the South Tropic line (Tropic of Capricorn).
4. What is the Great Rift Valley?
5. What five countries share waters of the Niger River?

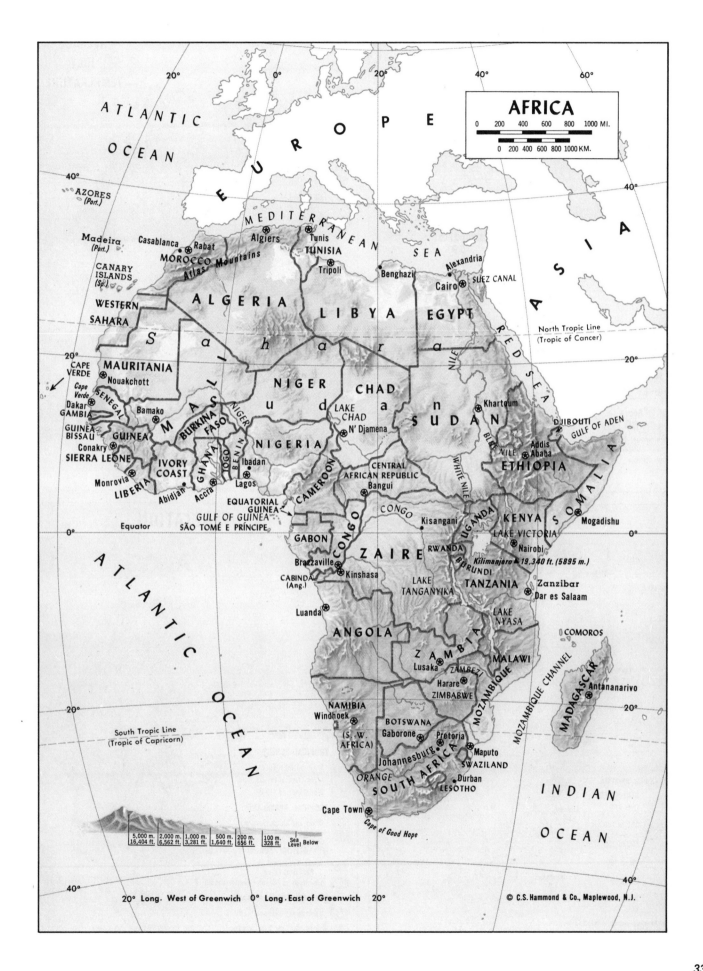

ATLANTIC OCEAN

EUROPE

ASIA

MEDITERRANEAN SEA

AZORES (Port.)

Madeira (Port.)

CANARY ISLANDS (Sp.)

Casablanca
Rabat
MOROCCO
Atlas Mountains
Algiers
Tunis
TUNISIA
Tripoli
Benghazi
Alexandria
Cairo
SUEZ CANAL

WESTERN SAHARA

ALGERIA
LIBYA
EGYPT

North Tropic Line (Tropic of Cancer)

CAPE VERDE
Cape Verde
Dakar
GAMBIA
GUINEA-BISSAU
Conakry
SIERRA LEONE
Monrovia
LIBERIA

MAURITANIA
Nouakchott
Bamako
SENEGAL
MALI
BURKINA FASO
GUINEA
IVORY COAST
GHANA
TOGO
BENIN
Abidjan
Accra
Lagos
Ibadan

Sahara

NIGER
NIGERIA
NIGER
LAKE CHAD
N'Djamena
CHAD
Sudan

Khartoum
BLUE NILE
DJIBOUTI
GULF OF ADEN
Addis Ababa
ETHIOPIA

SUDAN

NILE
RED SEA

EQUATORIAL GUINEA
GULF OF GUINEA
SÃO TOMÉ E PRÍNCIPE
CAMEROON
CENTRAL AFRICAN REPUBLIC
Bangui
Kisangani
WHITE NILE
UGANDA
LAKE VICTORIA
Nairobi
KENYA
SOMALIA
Mogadishu

Equator

GABON
CONGO
Brazzaville
CABINDA (Ang.)
Kinshasa
ZAIRE
CONGO
RWANDA
BURUNDI
Kilimanjaro ▲ 19,340 ft. (5895 m.)
TANZANIA
LAKE TANGANYIKA
Zanzibar
Dar es Salaam

Luanda

ATLANTIC OCEAN

ANGOLA
LAKE NYASA
ZAMBIA
Lusaka
MALAWI
ZAMBEZI
Harare
ZIMBABWE
MOZAMBIQUE
COMOROS
MADAGASCAR
Antananarivo
MOZAMBIQUE CHANNEL

South Tropic Line (Tropic of Capricorn)

NAMIBIA
Windhoek
(S.W. AFRICA)
BOTSWANA
Gaborone
Pretoria
Johannesburg
Maputo
SWAZILAND
ORANGE
SOUTH AFRICA
Durban
LESOTHO

Cape Town
Cape of Good Hope

INDIAN OCEAN

AFRICA

0 200 400 600 800 1000 MI.
0 200 400 600 800 1000 KM.

5,000 m. 16,404 ft. | 2,000 m. 6,562 ft. | 1,000 m. 3,281 ft. | 500 m. 1,640 ft. | 200 m. 656 ft. | 100 m. 328 ft. | Sea Level | Below

20° Long. West of Greenwich   0° Long. East of Greenwich   20°

© C.S. Hammond & Co., Maplewood, N.J.

33

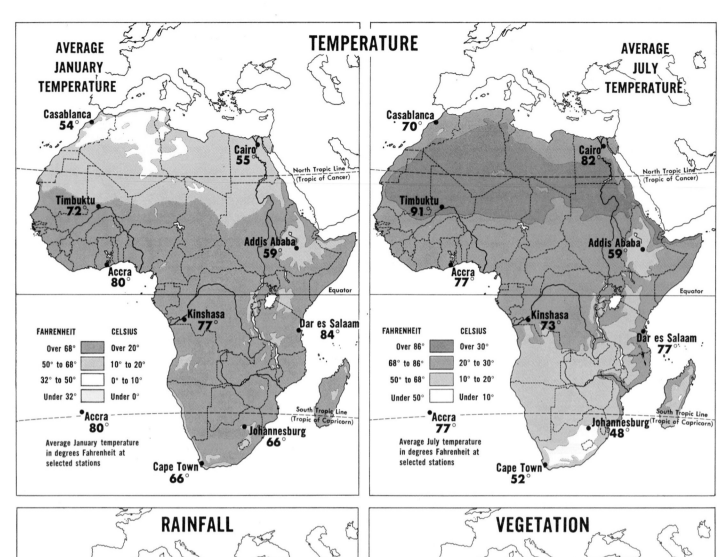

TEMPERATURE

AVERAGE JANUARY TEMPERATURE

Casablanca 54°
Cairo 55
Timbuktu 72
Addis Ababa 59
Accra 80°
Kinshasa 77°
Dar es Salaam 84°
Johannesburg 66°
Cape Town 66°

North Tropic Line (Tropic of Cancer)
Equator
South Tropic Line (Tropic of Capricorn)

FAHRENHEIT	CELSIUS
Over 68°	Over 20°
50° to 68°	10° to 20°
32° to 50°	0° to 10°
Under 32°	Under 0°

●Accra
80°

Average January temperature
in degrees Fahrenheit at
selected stations

AVERAGE JULY TEMPERATURE

Casablanca 70°
Cairo 82
Timbuktu 91
Addis Ababa 59
Accra 77°
Kinshasa 73°
Dar es Salaam 77°
Johannesburg 48°
Cape Town 52°

North Tropic Line (Tropic of Cancer)
Equator
South Tropic Line (Tropic of Capricorn)

FAHRENHEIT	CELSIUS
Over 86°	Over 30°
68° to 86°	20° to 30°
50° to 68°	10° to 20°
Under 50°	Under 10°

●Accra
77°

Average July temperature
in degrees Fahrenheit at
selected stations

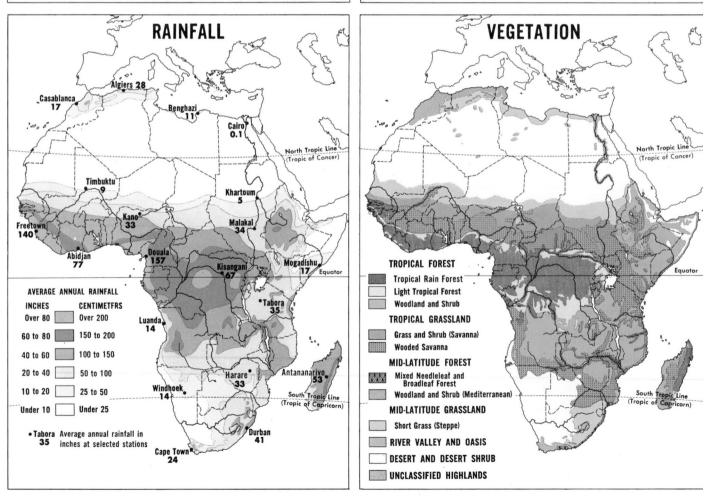

RAINFALL

Algiers 28
Casablanca 17
Benghazi 11
Cairo 0.1
Timbuktu 9
Khartoum 5
Kano 33
Freetown 140
Malakal 34
Abidjan 77
Douala 157
Kisangani 67
Mogadishu 17
Tabora 35
Luanda 14
Harare 33
Antananarivo 53
Windhoek 14
Durban 41
Cape Town 24

North Tropic Line (Tropic of Cancer)
Equator
South Tropic Line (Tropic of Capricorn)

AVERAGE ANNUAL RAINFALL

INCHES	CENTIMETERS
Over 80	Over 200
60 to 80	150 to 200
40 to 60	100 to 150
20 to 40	50 to 100
10 to 20	25 to 50
Under 10	Under 25

●Tabora Average annual rainfall in
35   inches at selected stations

VEGETATION

North Tropic Line (Tropic of Cancer)
Equator
South Tropic Line (Tropic of Capricorn)

TROPICAL FOREST
- Tropical Rain Forest
- Light Tropical Forest
- Woodland and Shrub

TROPICAL GRASSLAND
- Grass and Shrub (Savanna)
- Wooded Savanna

MID-LATITUDE FOREST
- Mixed Needleleaf and Broadleaf Forest
- Woodland and Shrub (Mediterranean)

MID-LATITUDE GRASSLAND
- Short Grass (Steppe)

RIVER VALLEY AND OASIS

DESERT AND DESERT SHRUB

UNCLASSIFIED HIGHLANDS

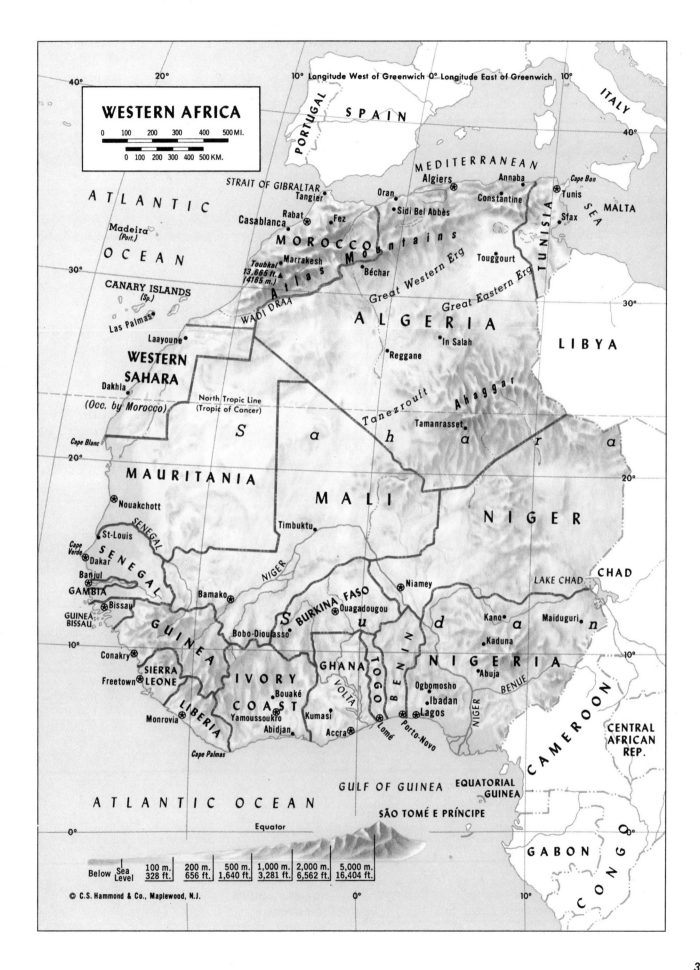

WESTERN AFRICA

0 100 200 300 400 500 MI.

0 100 200 300 400 500 KM.

40° 20° 10° Longitude West of Greenwich 0° Longitude East of Greenwich 10°

ITALY

PORTUGAL SPAIN

40°

ATLANTIC

MEDITERRANEAN

STRAIT OF GIBRALTAR Tangier Oran Algiers Annaba Cape Bon Tunis
Casablanca Rabat Fez Sidi Bel Abbès Constantine Sfax MALTA
Madeira (Port.) MOROCCO Marrakesh Béchar Touggourt TUNISIA SEA

OCEAN

Toubkal 13,665 ft. ▲ (4165 m.) Atlas Mountains
Great Western Erg Great Eastern Erg

30° CANARY ISLANDS (Sp.) 30°

WADI DRAA ALGERIA LIBYA

Las Palmas

Laayoune In Salah
Reggane

WESTERN
SAHARA North Tropic Line (Tropic of Cancer) Tanezrouft Ahaggar
Dakhla Tamanrasset

(Occ. by Morocco) S a h a r a

Cape Blanc 20° 20°

MAURITANIA

MALI NIGER

Nouakchott

St-Louis SENEGAL CHAD
Cape Verde Timbuktu LAKE CHAD

Dakar SENEGAL NIGER
Banjul Bamako Niamey
GAMBIA S BURKINA FASO u d a n Kano Maiduguri
Bissau Ouagadougou Kaduna
GUINEA-BISSAU GUINEA Bobo-Dioulasso NIGERIA
Conakry GHANA TOGO BENIN Abuja BENUE
SIERRA IVORY VOLTA Ogbomosho NIGER
Freetown LEONE COAST Bouaké Ibadan CAMEROON CENTRAL
Monrovia LIBERIA Yamoussoukro Kumasi Lagos AFRICAN
Abidjan Accra Lomé Porto-Novo REP.
Cape Palmas

GULF OF GUINEA EQUATORIAL GUINEA

ATLANTIC OCEAN SÃO TOMÉ E PRÍNCIPE GABON CONGO

Equator 0°

Below Sea Level | 100 m. 328 ft. | 200 m. 656 ft. | 500 m. 1,640 ft. | 1,000 m. 3,281 ft. | 2,000 m. 6,562 ft. | 5,000 m. 16,404 ft.

© C.S. Hammond & Co., Maplewood, N.J.

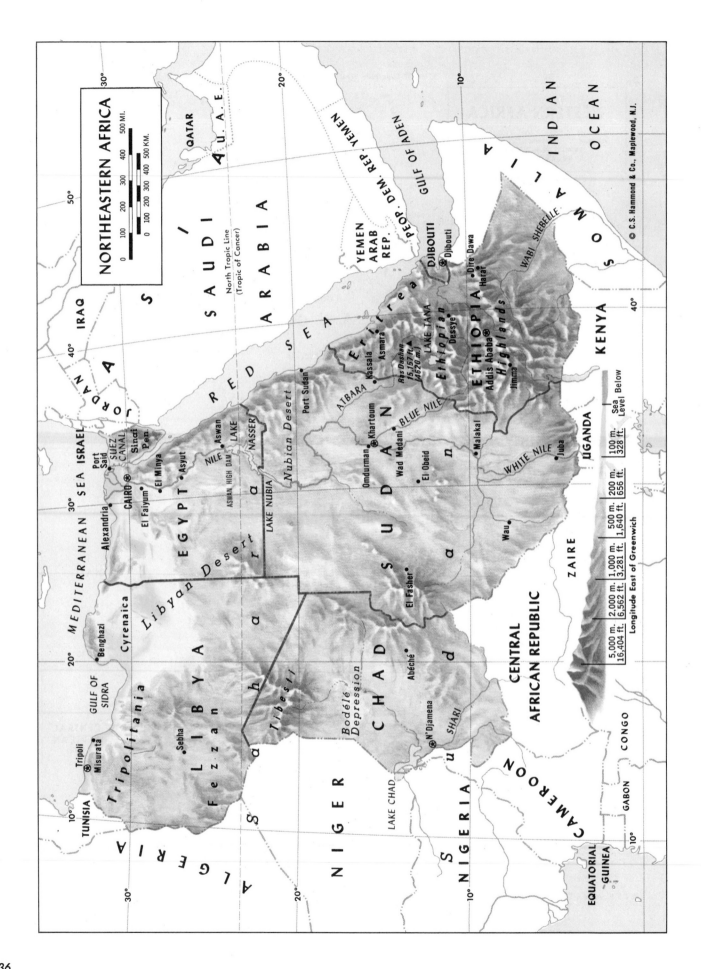

NORTHEASTERN AFRICA

500 MI.
400
300
200
100
0

0   100   200   300   400   500 KM.

North Tropic Line
(Tropic of Cancer)

QATAR
U.A.E.
SAUDI ARABIA
IRAQ
JORDAN
ISRAEL
MEDITERRANEAN SEA

YEMEN ARAB REP.
PEOP. DEM. REP. YEMEN
GULF OF ADEN

INDIAN OCEAN

© C.S. Hammond & Co., Maplewood, N.J.

SOMALIA

DJIBOUTI
Djibouti
Dire Dawa
Harar

Eritrea
Asmara
Kassala
Ras Dashan
15,157 ft.
(4620 m.)
LAKE TANA
Dessye

Ethiopian Highlands
ETHIOPIA
Addis Ababa
Jimma

WABI SHEBELLE

KENYA

RED SEA

Port Sudan
Nubian Desert
ATBARA
BLUE NILE
Khartoum
Omdurman
Wad Medani
El Obeid

SUDAN

Malakal
WHITE NILE
Juba

UGANDA

Sea Level
Below
100 m.
328 ft.

200 m.
656 ft.

500 m.
1,640 ft.

1,000 m.
3,281 ft.

2,000 m.
6,562 ft.

5,000 m.
16,404 ft.

Longitude East of Greenwich

Port Said
SUEZ CANAL
Sinai Pen.
Aswan
LAKE NASSER
NILE
Asyut
El Minya
Aswan High Dam
LAKE NUBIA
CAIRO
El Faiyum
Alexandria

EGYPT

Sahara

Libyan Desert

Wau

ZAIRE

CENTRAL AFRICAN REPUBLIC

CONGO

GABON

EQUATORIAL GUINEA

CAMEROON

NIGERIA

Benghazi
Cyrenaica
GULF OF SIDRA
Tripoli
Misurata
Tripolitania
LIBYA
Fezzan
Sebha
Tibesti

Bodélé Depression

El Fasher

CHAD

Abéché

N'Djamena
SHARI

LAKE CHAD

NIGER

ALGERIA

TUNISIA

30°
20°
10°
50°
40°
20°
30°
20°
10°
10°
40°
10°

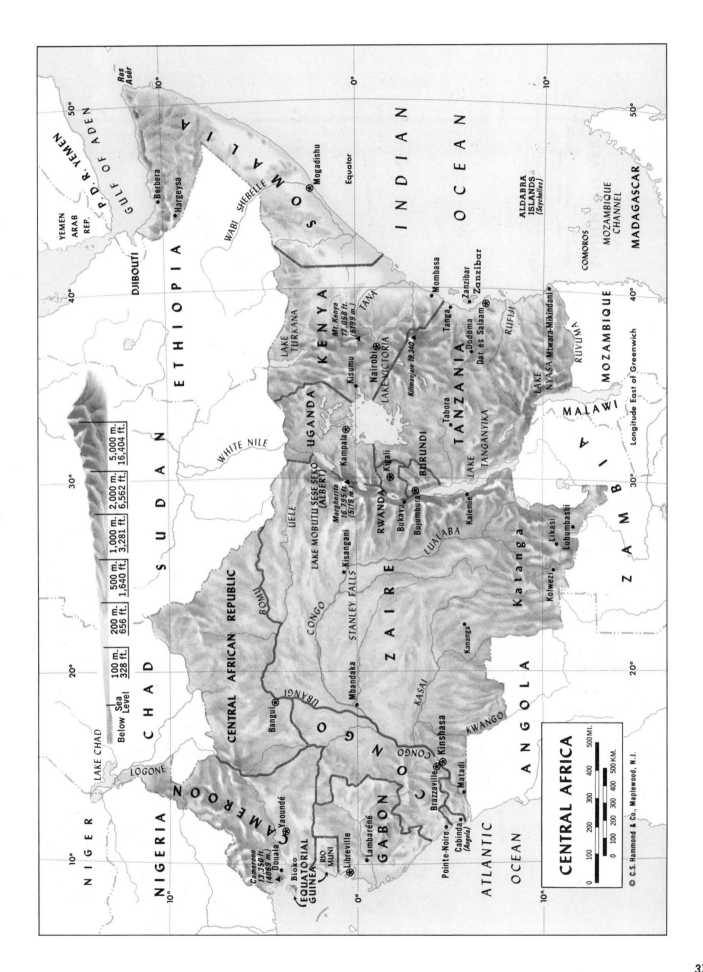

CENTRAL AFRICA

© C.S. Hammond & Co., Maplewood, N.J.

100 200 300 400 500 MI.

0 100 200 300 400 500 KM.

5,000 m. 16,404 ft.
2,000 m. 6,562 ft.
1,000 m. 3,281 ft.
500 m. 1,640 ft.
200 m. 656 ft.
100 m. 328 ft.
Sea Level
Below

YEMEN ARAB REP.

P.D.R. YEMEN

GULF OF ADEN

DJIBOUTI

ETHIOPIA

SOMALIA

Ras Asér

Berbera
Hargeysa

Mogadishu

WABI SHEBELLE

INDIAN OCEAN

Equator

ALDABRA ISLANDS (Seychelles)

COMOROS

MOZAMBIQUE CHANNEL

MADAGASCAR

Longitude East of Greenwich

MOZAMBIQUE

MALAWI

ZAMBIA

SUDAN

CHAD

NIGER

NIGERIA

LAKE CHAD

LOGONE

CAMEROON

Cameroon 13,350 ft. (4069 m.)

Bioko

Douala
Yaoundé

EQUATORIAL GUINEA

RIO MUNI

Libreville

Lambaréné

GABON

CONGO

Pointe-Noire

Cabinda (Angola)

Brazzaville

Matadi

Kinshasa

CONGO

KWANGO

KASAI

ANGOLA

ATLANTIC OCEAN

CENTRAL AFRICAN REPUBLIC

BOMU

UBANGI

Bangui

UELE

CONGO

Kisangani

STANLEY FALLS

ZAIRE

Mbandaka

Kananga

Kolwezi

Katanga

Likasi

Lubumbashi

LUALABA

LAKE MOBUTU SESE SEKO (ALBERT)

WHITE NILE

UGANDA

Kampala

Margherita 16,795 ft. (5119 m.)

RWANDA

Kigali

BURUNDI

Bukavu

Bujumbura

LAKE TANGANYIKA

Kalemie

Tabora

TANZANIA

Dodoma

Dar es Salaam

RUFIJI

LAKE NYASA

RUVUMA

Mtwara-Mikindani

Tanga

Zanzibar

Zanzibar

Mombasa

KENYA

LAKE TURKANA

Mt. Kenya 17,058 ft. (5199 m.)

TANA

Kisumu

Nairobi

LAKE VICTORIA

Kilimanjaro 19,340

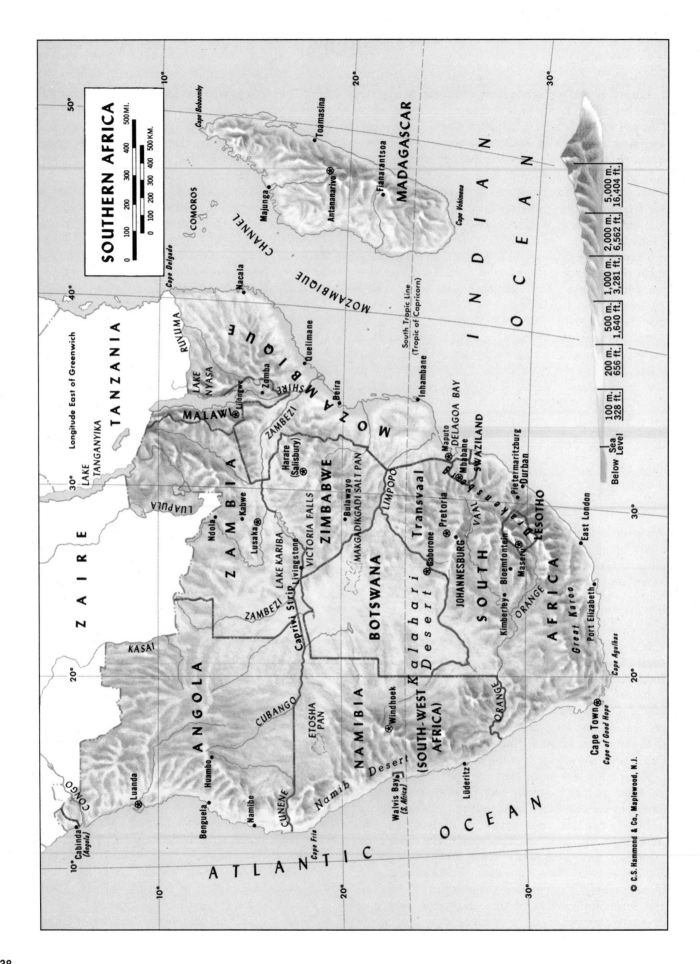

SOUTHERN AFRICA

500 MI.
500 KM.

5,000 m. 16,404 ft.
2,000 m. 6,562 ft.
1,000 m. 3,281 ft.
500 m. 1,640 ft.
200 m. 656 ft.
100 m. 328 ft.
Below Sea Level

Longitude East of Greenwich

INDIAN OCEAN

MOZAMBIQUE CHANNEL

MADAGASCAR

Cape Bobaomby
•Toamasina
Majunga•
Antananarivo⊕
•Fianarantsoa
Cape Vohimena

COMOROS

Cape Delgado
•Nacala

RUVUMA

TANZANIA

LAKE TANGANYIKA
LAKE NYASA

MALAWI⊕
Lilongwe•
•Zomba

MOZAMBIQUE

•Quelimane
•Beira

ZAMBEZI
SHIRE

South Tropic Line (Tropic of Capricorn)

•Inhambane

DELAGOA BAY
Maputo•
•Mbabane
SWAZILAND

ZAIRE

LUAPULA

Harare (Salisbury)⊕
ZIMBABWE
Bulawayo•

ZAMBIA
•Ndola
Kabwe•
Lusaka⊕
LAKE KARIBA
VICTORIA FALLS
Livingstone•

MAKGADIKGADI SALT PAN

Transvaal
Pretoria⊕

VAAL
Pietermaritzburg•
•Durban

Drakensberg
LESOTHO
Maseru⊕
•East London

KASAI

Caprivi Strip
ZAMBEZI

BOTSWANA
Gaborone⊕
Kalahari Desert

JOHANNESBURG⊕

Kimberley•
Bloemfontein•
ORANGE

SOUTH AFRICA

Great Karoo
•Port Elizabeth
Cape Agulhas

ANGOLA
Luanda•

CUBANGO

ETOSHA PAN

NAMIBIA
(SOUTH-WEST AFRICA)
Windhoek⊕

ORANGE

CONGO
Cabinda (Angola)

Benguela•
Namibe•
CUNENE
Cape Frio

Namib Desert

Walvis Bay (S. Africa)
•Lüderitz

Cape Town⊕
Cape of Good Hope

ATLANTIC OCEAN

Huambo•

© C.S. Hammond & Co., Maplewood, N.J.

EUROPE

Europe is the second-smallest continent. Only Australia is smaller. If you look at the map, you will notice that you cannot tell from the shape where Europe ends and Asia begins. That is because there is no natural boundary between the two. Europe and Asia make up a large landmass known as *Eurasia*. People have traditionally drawn the boundary between the two along the Ural Mountains and Ural River to the Caspian Sea, and then westward along the border of the Soviet Union to the Black Sea.

Europe is well shaped and situated for the development of sea trade. It has a very irregular shape. The number of large inlets of the ocean and of large peninsulas—and the fact that Europe itself is really a very large peninsula of Asia—means that no part of Europe is very far from the sea. Many places along its very indented coastline are natural harbors, and many of them are at the mouths of long rivers that run into the continent. Find the Thames, Rhine, Elbe, Seine, and the Tagus on the maps.

In the north, near the North and Baltic Seas, are the Scandinavian and Jutland peninsulas. Norway and Sweden occupy Scandinavia, and Denmark is on Jutland. Finland is often considered part of Scandinavia although it is not actually on the peninsula. To the southwest is the Iberian Peninsula on which Spain and Portugal are located. Italy thrusts into the Mediterranean Sea and the Balkan Peninsula is to its east. Study the positions of the peninsulas along the North Atlantic Ocean and the Mediterranean. Both bodies of water are major highways of world trade. Ships constantly cross the Atlantic to North and South America. Those bound for Asia sail across the Mediterranean and through the Suez Canal and the Red Sea to the east.

Many large islands and island groups are off the coast. The largest are the British Isles, which include Ireland. These islands are in the same latitude as Labrador in North America, but they have a much milder climate because the water and winds in the eastern Atlantic are warm. Farther out in the Atlantic is the island of Iceland, Europe's westernmost nation. Other large islands are in the Mediterranean Sea.

Europe has few areas that have not been cultivated or where people have not settled. Few areas do not have mineral resources. Coal and iron are important.

Europe has four major regions. They are the Northwest Highlands, the Great European Plain, the Central Highlands, and the Alpine System. The extreme northwestern region, the Northwest Highlands, extends through northwestern France, the northern British Isles, and Scandinavia. Parts of these highlands were once covered by huge glaciers, or sheets of ice, during the ice ages. These glaciers carved deep paths, or fiords, through the mountains on their way to the sea. In some places they carried away the soil. Therefore, much of this region is not good for agriculture. Where possible, people have used this land for grazing. Many of the people have turned to the sea for a living.

The Great European or Central Plain stretches from the Atlantic coast of France eastward to the Ural Mountains. It includes southern England and southern Sweden. In the Soviet Union, these plains extend from the Arctic south to the Caspian Sea. Near the Arctic the plain is called *tundra*—a cold, flat region where the soil is frozen much of the time and where only a few low plants will grow. Sections of this plain in western Europe and the southern part of the Soviet Union are some of the world's richest farmlands. In the lowlands of this plain, people have had to build dikes and dams to prevent the area from being drowned by the sea.

South of the Great European Plain are the Central Highlands. This region begins at the Massif Central, a plateau in central France, and it stretches eastward to the Soviet Union. These highlands are very heavily forested. In all of these and other highland regions of Europe, there are many small plains and plateaus that are important agricultural areas.

The Alpine Mountain System covers much of southern Europe and is famous for its great beauty. The mountains extend from Spain eastward to the Caspian Sea. Its principal ranges are the Sierra Nevada, Pyrenees, Alps, Apennines, Carpathians, Balkans, and Caucasus. Mont Blanc, 15,771 feet (4,807 meters) above sea level, is the highest point in the Alps. Mt. Elbrus, in the Caucasus, is the highest point in Europe at 18,510 feet (5,642 meters) above sea level. Geographers who do not consider the Caucasus as part of Europe but as the southwestern boundary of Asia, do not consider Mt. Elbrus to be the highest point in Europe.

Generally Europe has a mild, temperate climate, and most of it receives adequate rainfall. In eastern and northern Europe and the central part of the Iberian Peninsula, there are greater extremes of temperature.

---

1. What three capital cities lie on the Danube River? What countries are they the capitals of?
2. What two countries lie partly in Europe and partly in Asia?
3. What do the capitals of Iceland, Norway, Sweden, Denmark, and Finland have in common?
4. What are the four natural land regions of Europe?

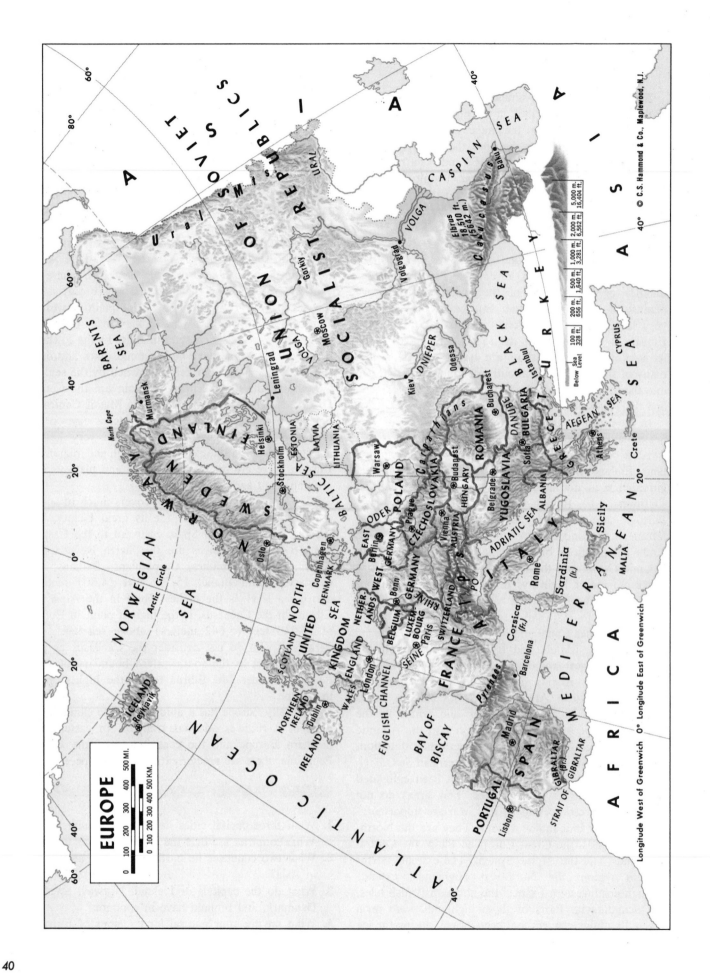

EUROPE

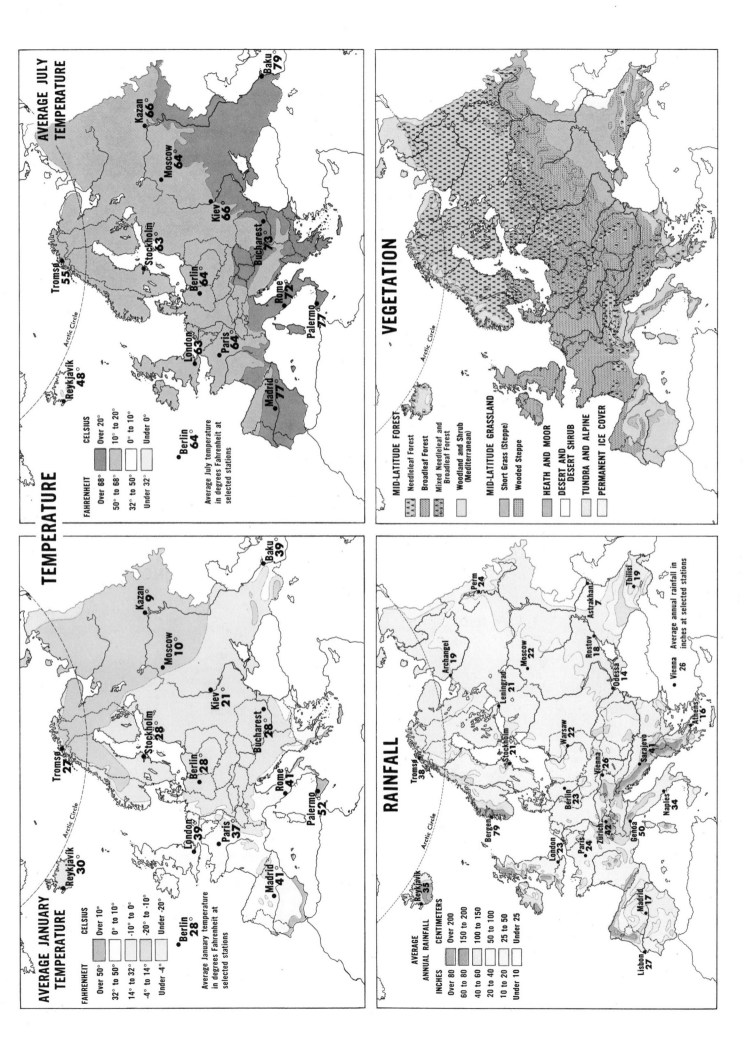

TEMPERATURE

AVERAGE JANUARY TEMPERATURE

FAHRENHEIT	CELSIUS
Over 50°	Over 10°
32° to 50°	0° to 10°
14° to 32°	-10° to 0°
-4° to 14°	-20° to -10°
Under -4°	Under -20°

• Berlin
28°

Average January temperature in degrees Fahrenheit at selected stations

Arctic Circle

Reykjavik 30°
Tromsø 22°
Kazan 9°
Moscow 10°
Stockholm 28°
Kiev 21°
London 39°
Berlin 28°
Bucharest 28°
Paris 37°
Rome 41°
Madrid 41°
Palermo 52°
Baku 39°

AVERAGE JULY TEMPERATURE

FAHRENHEIT	CELSIUS
Over 68°	Over 20°
50° to 68°	10° to 20°
32° to 50°	0° to 10°
Under 32°	Under 0°

• Berlin
64°

Average July temperature in degrees Fahrenheit at selected stations

Arctic Circle

Baku 79°
Kazan 66°
Moscow 64°
Kiev 66°
Stockholm 63°
Tromsø 55°
Reykjavik 48°
Bucharest 73°
Berlin 64°
London 63°
Paris 64°
Rome 72°
Palermo 77°
Madrid 77°

RAINFALL

INCHES	AVERAGE ANNUAL RAINFALL CENTIMETERS
Over 80	Over 200
60 to 80	150 to 200
40 to 60	100 to 150
20 to 40	50 to 100
10 to 20	25 to 50
Under 10	Under 25

• Vienna
26

Average annual rainfall in inches at selected stations

Arctic Circle

Perm 24
Archangel 19
Astrakhan 7
Tromsø 38
Leningrad 21
Moscow 22
Rostov 18
Tbilisi 19
Bergen 79
Stockholm 21
Warsaw 22
Odessa 14
Reykjavik 35
London 23
Berlin 23
Vienna 26
Sarajevo 41
Athens 16
Paris 24
Zürich 42
Genoa 50
Naples 34
Madrid 17
Lisbon 27

VEGETATION

MID-LATITUDE FOREST
- Needleleaf Forest
- Broadleaf Forest
- Mixed Needleleaf and Broadleaf Forest
- Woodland and Shrub (Mediterranean)

MID-LATITUDE GRASSLAND
- Short Grass (Steppe)
- Wooded Steppe

- HEATH AND MOOR
- DESERT AND DESERT SHRUB
- TUNDRA AND ALPINE
- PERMANENT ICE COVER

Arctic Circle

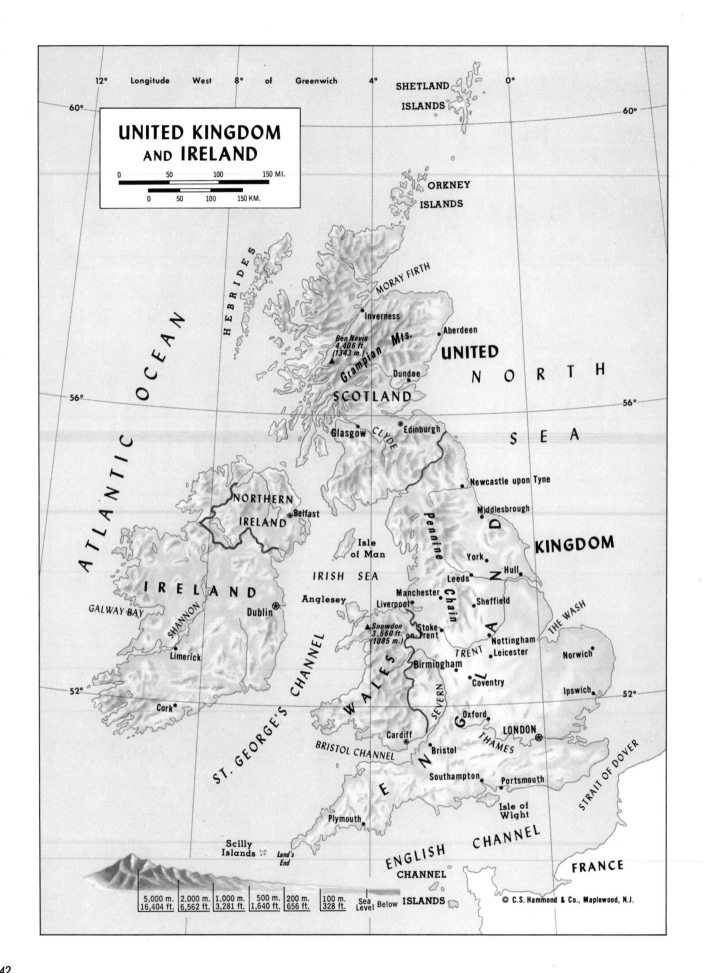

UNITED KINGDOM AND IRELAND

0   50   100   150 MI.

0   50   100   150 KM.

Longitude   West   of   Greenwich

SHETLAND ISLANDS

ORKNEY ISLANDS

HEBRIDES

ATLANTIC OCEAN

MORAY FIRTH

Inverness

Ben Nevis 4,406 ft. (1343 m.)

Grampian Mts.

Aberdeen

UNITED

Dundee

SCOTLAND

NORTH

Glasgow   CLYDE   Edinburgh

SEA

Newcastle upon Tyne

Middlesbrough

NORTHERN IRELAND

Belfast

Isle of Man

Pennine Chain

KINGDOM

York

Hull

IRISH SEA

Leeds

IRELAND

Anglesey

Manchester

Sheffield

GALWAY BAY

SHANNON

Dublin

Liverpool

Stoke-on-Trent

Nottingham

THE WASH

Snowdon 3,560 ft. (1085 m.)

TRENT

Leicester

Norwich

Limerick

Birmingham

ST. GEORGE'S CHANNEL

WALES

Coventry

Ipswich

Cork

SEVERN

Oxford

LONDON

Cardiff

Bristol

THAMES

BRISTOL CHANNEL

ENGLAND

Southampton

Portsmouth

STRAIT OF DOVER

Plymouth

Isle of Wight

Scilly Islands   Land's End

ENGLISH CHANNEL

CHANNEL   FRANCE

CHANNEL ISLANDS

© C.S. Hammond & Co., Maplewood, N.J.

5,000 m. 16,404 ft. | 2,000 m. 6,562 ft. | 1,000 m. 3,281 ft. | 500 m. 1,640 ft. | 200 m. 656 ft. | 100 m. 328 ft. | Sea Level | Below

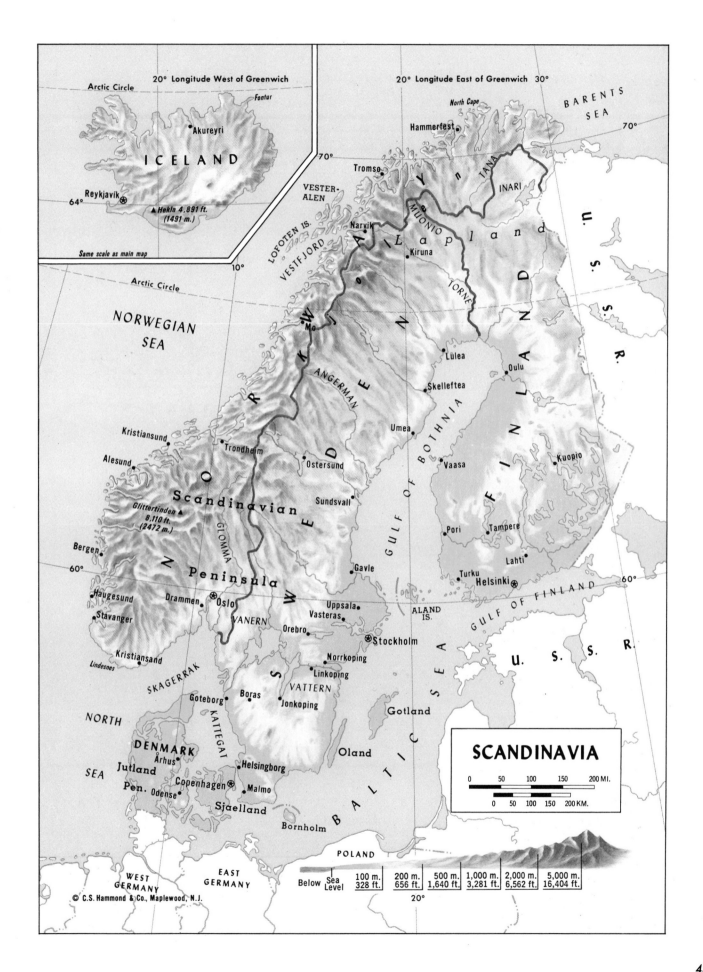

20° Longitude West of Greenwich

20° Longitude East of Greenwich 30°

Fontur

BARENTS SEA

70°

North Cape

Hammerfest

70°

• Akureyri

ICELAND

VESTER-
ALEN

Tromso •

TANA

INARI

U.

64°

Reykjavík ⊗

▲ *Hekla 4,891 ft.
(1491 m.)*

10°

LOFOTEN IS.

VESTFJORD

• Narvik

Y   n

MUONIO

L a p l a n d

S.

Same scale as main map

Arctic Circle

Kiruna •

TORNE

S.

NORWEGIAN
SEA

R

o

Mo

Lulea •

R.

Oulu •

W

Skelleftea •

E

ANGERMAN

Kristiansund •

• Trondheim

Umea •

D

Alesund •

• Ostersund

GULF OF BOTHNIA

Vaasa •

F

Kuopio •

O

Scandinavian

Sundsvall •

E

I

Glittertinden ▲
8,110 ft.
(2472 m.)

N

Pori •

Tampere •

L

Bergen •

GLOMMA

60°

Gavle •

Lahti •

A

Haugesund •

Peninsula

W

Turku •

Helsinki ⊗

60°

Drammen •   • Oslo ⊗

Uppsala •

ALAND
IS.

GULF OF FINLAND

Stavanger •

VANERN

Vasteras •

N

Orebro •

⊗ Stockholm

D

Kristiansand •

S

Norrkoping •

Lindesnes

Linkoping •

U.   S.   S.   R.

SKAGERRAK

E

VATTERN

Boras •

Goteborg •

Jonkoping •

Gotland

NORTH

W

KATTEGAT

DENMARK

Oland

BALTIC   SEA

SEA

Arhus •

Helsingborg •

SCANDINAVIA

Jutland

Copenhagen ⊗   • Malmo

| 0 | 50 | 100 | 150 | 200 MI. |

Pen.   Odense •

| 0 | 50 | 100 | 150 | 200 KM. |

Sjaelland

Bornholm

POLAND

WEST
GERMANY

EAST
GERMANY

Below   Sea
Level

100 m.
328 ft.

200 m.
656 ft.

500 m.
1,640 ft.

1,000 m.
3,281 ft.

2,000 m.
6,562 ft.

5,000 m.
16,404 ft.

20°

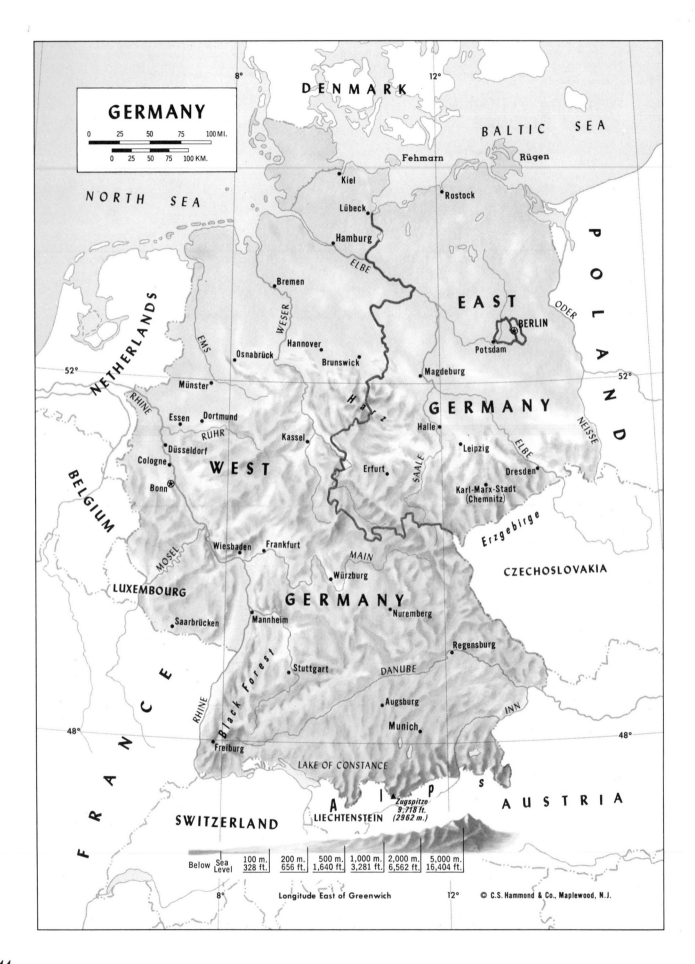

DENMARK

BALTIC SEA

NORTH SEA

GERMANY

0   25   50   75   100 MI.
0   25   50   75   100 KM.

Fehmarn

Rügen

Kiel

Rostock

Lübeck

Hamburg

ELBE

Bremen

WESER

EAST

BERLIN

ODER

Potsdam

EMS

Hannover

NETHERLANDS

Osnabrück

Brunswick

GERMANY

52°

Magdeburg

52°

Münster

RHINE

Halle

Harz

NEISSE

Essen   Dortmund

RUHR

Kassel

Leipzig

ELBE

Düsseldorf

Cologne

WEST

Erfurt

SAALE

Dresden

Bonn

Karl-Marx-Stadt
(Chemnitz)

BELGIUM

Erzgebirge

Wiesbaden   Frankfurt

MOSEL

MAIN

CZECHOSLOVAKIA

Würzburg

LUXEMBOURG

GERMANY

Saarbrücken

Mannheim

Nuremberg

Regensburg

Stuttgart

DANUBE

Black Forest

RHINE

Augsburg

INN

Munich

FRANCE

48°

48°

Freiburg

LAKE OF CONSTANCE

Zugspitze
9,718 ft.
(2962 m.)

A L P s

AUSTRIA

SWITZERLAND

LIECHTENSTEIN

Below Sea
Level

100 m.
328 ft.

200 m.
656 ft.

500 m.
1,640 ft.

1,000 m.
3,281 ft.

2,000 m.
6,562 ft.

5,000 m.
16,404 ft.

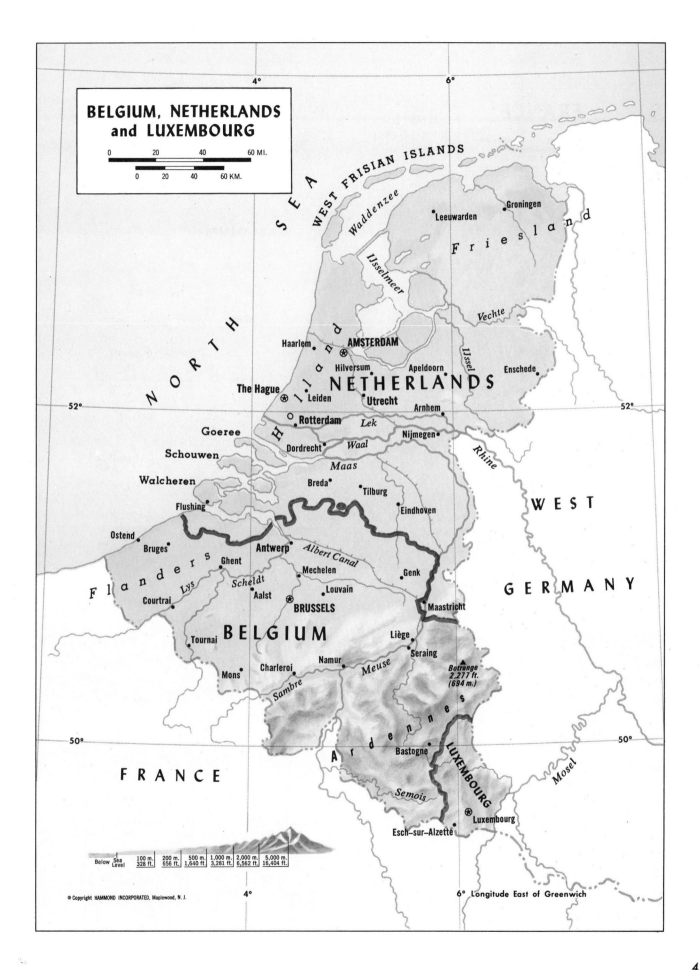

BELGIUM, NETHERLANDS and LUXEMBOURG

0   20   40   60 MI.

0   20   40   60 KM.

N O R T H   S E A

WEST FRISIAN ISLANDS

Waddenzee

Leeuwarden
Groningen

F r i e s l a n d

IJsselmeer

Vechte

Haarlem
AMSTERDAM
Hilversum
Apeldoorn
Enschede

The Hague
Leiden
Utrecht

NETHERLANDS

IJssel

52°   52°

Arnhem

Goeree

Rotterdam
Lek

H o l l a n d

Rhine

Schouwen

Dordrecht
Waal

Nijmegen

Maas

Walcheren

Breda
Tilburg

W E S T

Flushing

Eindhoven

Ostend
Bruges

Antwerp
Albert Canal

Ghent
Mechelen
Genk

F l a n d e r s

Scheldt
Louvain

G E R M A N Y

Lys
Aalst

Courtrai

BRUSSELS

Maastricht

BELGIUM

Tournai

Liège
Seraing

Mons
Charleroi
Namur
Meuse

▲ Botrange
2,277 ft.
(694 m.)

Sambre

A r d e n n e s

50°   50°

Bastogne
LUXEMBOURG

F R A N C E

Semois

Mosel

Luxembourg

Esch–sur–Alzette

Below Sea
Level
100 m.
328 ft.
200 m.
656 ft.
500 m.
1,640 ft.
1,000 m.
3,281 ft.
2,000 m.
6,562 ft.
5,000 m.
16,404 ft.

4°

6° Longitude East of Greenwich

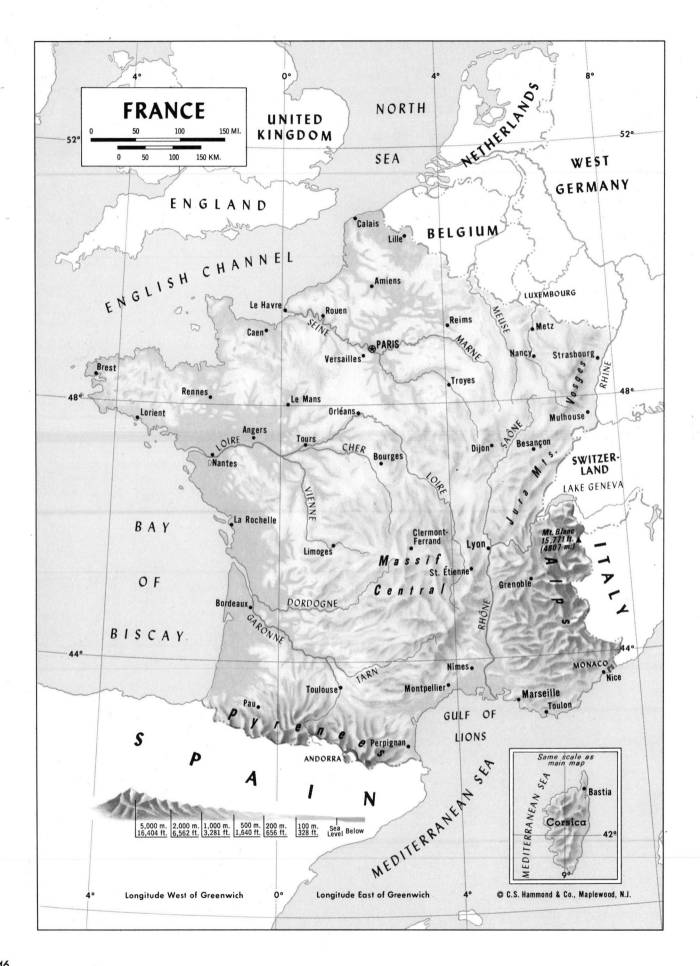

FRANCE

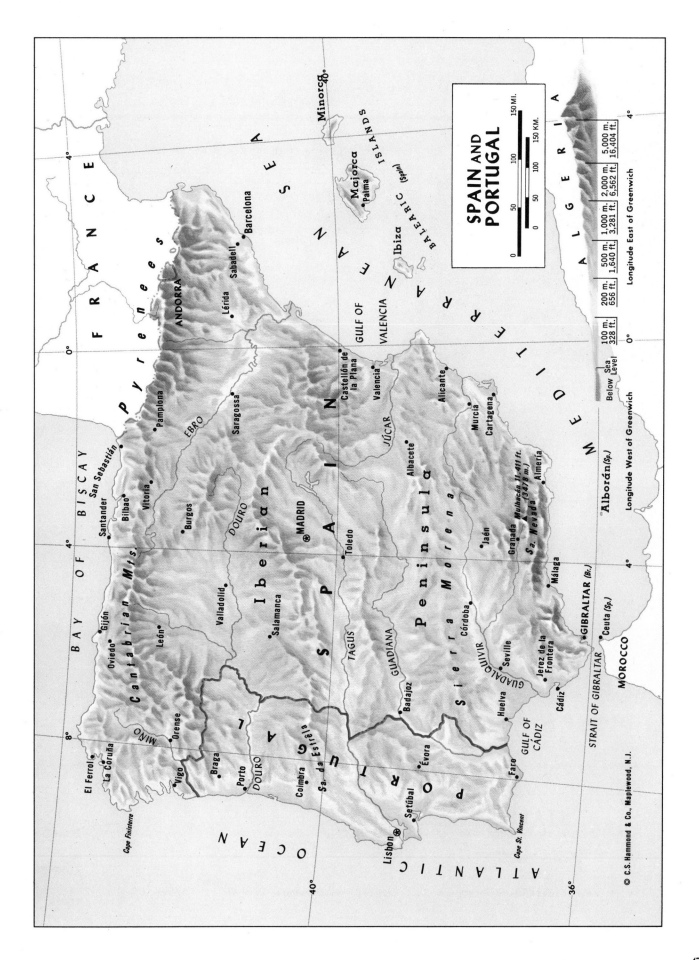

SPAIN AND PORTUGAL

150 MI.
150 KM.

5,000 m.	16,404 ft.	
2,000 m.	6,562 ft.	
1,000 m.	3,281 ft.	
500 m.	1,640 ft.	
200 m.	656 ft.	
100 m.	328 ft.	
Sea Level		
Below		

Longitude East of Greenwich

FRANCE

Pyrenees

ANDORRA

Barcelona
Sabadell
Lérida
Pamplona
EBRO
Saragossa

MINORCA
Majorca
Palma
IBIZA
BALEARIC ISLANDS (Spain)

BAY OF BISCAY

San Sebastián
Santander
Bilbao
Vitoria
Burgos

Castellón de la Plana
Valencia
GULF OF VALENCIA
JÚCAR

Alicante
Murcia
Cartagena

Cantabrian Mts.

Gijón
Oviedo
León
Valladolid
Salamanca

Iberian

DOURO

MADRID
Toledo

SPAIN

Albacete

Almería
Granada Mulhacén 11,411 ft. (3,478 m.)
Sa. Nevada

MEDITERRANEAN SEA

ALGERIA

Alborán (Sp.)
Longitude West of Greenwich

El Ferrol
La Coruña
Cape Finisterre
Vigo
MIÑO
Orense

Braga
Porto
DOURO
Coimbra
Sa. da Estrela

TAGUS
GUADIANA
Sierra Morena
Córdoba
Jaén
Málaga
GIBRALTAR (B.J.)
Ceuta (Sp.)

Peninsula

Badajoz
Évora
Setúbal

PORTUGAL

Lisbon

GUADALQUIVIR
Seville
Jerez de la Frontera
Huelva
Cádiz
GULF OF CÁDIZ
STRAIT OF GIBRALTAR
MOROCCO

Faro
Cape St. Vincent

ATLANTIC OCEAN

© C.S. Hammond & Co., Maplewood, N.J.

47

48°   8°   12°   16°   48°

| 5,000 m. | 2,000 m. | 1,000 m. | 500 m. | 200 m. | 100 m. | Sea | |
| 16,404 ft. | 6,562 ft. | 3,281 ft. | 1,640 ft. | 656 ft. | 328 ft. | Level | Below |

LIECHTENSTEIN

AUSTRIA

HUNGARY

SWITZERLAND

A   L   P   S

Mte. Rosa
15,203 ft.
(4634 m.)▲

Trento

Trieste

Brescia•
  •Padua

Milan•   Verona•

ADIGE

Venice•

Turin•

PO

YUGOSLAVIA

A   P   P   E   N   N

Parma•   PO
   •Ferrara

Genoa•   •Bologna

44°   44°

Florence•

D

ADRIATIC

ARNO

SAN
MARINO

LIGURIAN

Leghorn•

Ancona•

SEA

•Siena

Elba

n

Viterbo•   TIBER

Pescara•

C

VATICAN CITY⊕
    ⊛ROME

Corsica
(Fr.)

n

•Latina

Foggia•

SEA

TYRRHENIAN

•Bari

Vesuvius
4,190 ft.
(1277 m.)▲

Naples•

Taranto•

•Salerno

Sardinia

40°   40°

SEA

GULF OF
TARANTO

s

Cagliari•

IONIAN

Messina•

MEDITERRANEAN

Palermo•

•Reggio di Calabria

SEA

Etna 11,053 ft.
(3369 m.)▲

Sicily   •Catania

SEA

Pantelleria

C. Passero

ITALY

| 0 | 50 | 100 | 150 MI. |

| 0 | 50 | 100 | 150 KM. |

36°   36°

MALTA

8°   12°   Longitude East of Greenwich   16°

F R A N C E

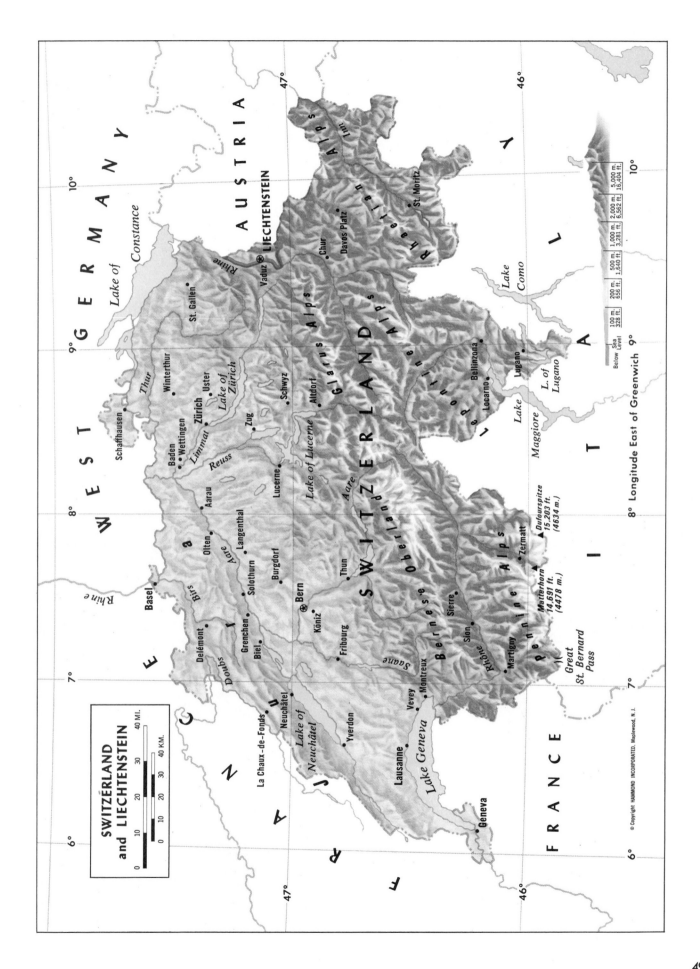

SWITZERLAND and LIECHTENSTEIN

40 MI.

40 KM.

W E S T   G E R M A N Y

A U S T R I A

LIECHTENSTEIN

Lake of Constance

Rhine

Schaffhausen

St. Gallen

Winterthur

Uster

Thur

Zürich

Lake of Zürich

Baden

Wettingen

Limmat

Zürich

Zug

Schwyz

Altdorf

Vaduz

Chur

Davos Platz

St. Moritz

Rhaetian Alps

Glarus Alps

Aarau

Reuss

Lucerne

Lake of Lucerne

Aare

Olten

Langenthal

Burgdorf

Solothurn

Bern

Köniz

Fribourg

Thun

Berner Oberland Alps

Basel

Birs

Delémont

Grenchen

Biel

Doubs

Neuchâtel

Lake of Neuchâtel

La Chaux-de-Fonds

Yverdon

Vevey

Montreux

Saane

Saane

Sierre

Sion

Rhône

Martigny

Bernese Alps

Pennine Alps

Great St. Bernard Pass

Zermatt

▲ Dufourspitze 15,203 ft. (4634 m.)

▲ Matterhorn 14,691 ft. (4478 m.)

Lake Geneva

Lausanne

Geneva

J U R A

F R A N C E

I T A L Y

Bellinzona

Locarno

Lugano

L. of Lugano

Lake Maggiore

Lake Como

Lepontine Alps

S W I T Z E R L A N D

Rhine

Inn

10°

9°

8°

7°

6°

47°

46°

10°

9°

8°

7°

6°

47°

46°

8° Longitude East of Greenwich 9°

100 m. 328 ft.

200 m. 656 ft.

500 m. 1,640 ft.

1,000 m. 3,281 ft.

2,000 m. 6,562 ft.

5,000 m. 16,404 ft.

Below Sea Level

Sea Level

© Copyright HAMMOND INCORPORATED, Maplewood, N.J.

49

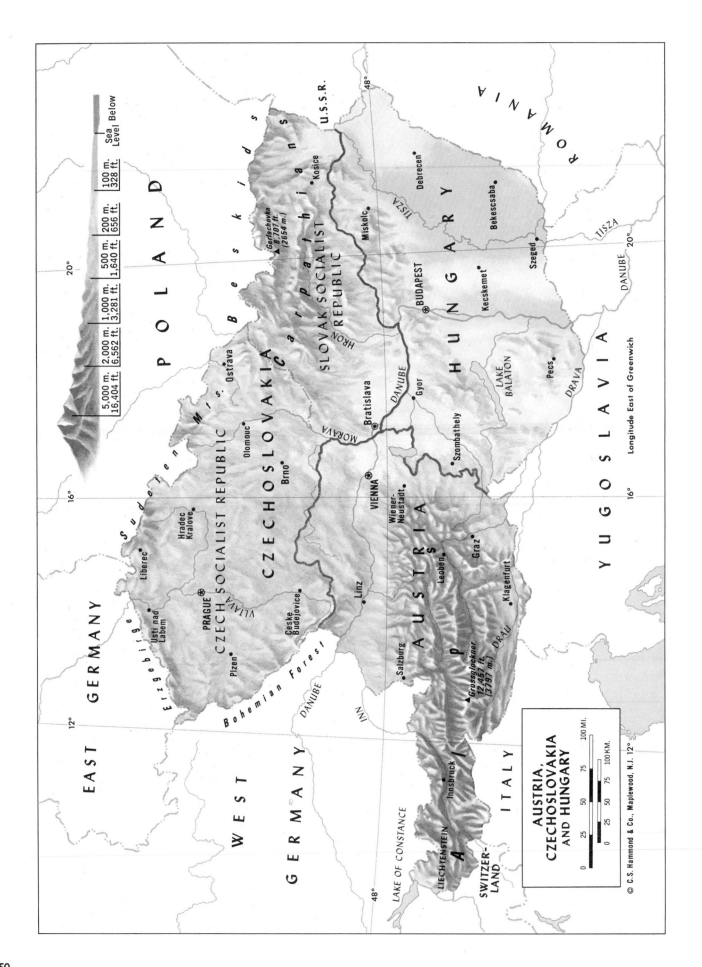

POLAND

EAST GERMANY

WEST GERMANY

CZECHOSLOVAKIA

CZECH SOCIALIST REPUBLIC

SLOVAK SOCIALIST REPUBLIC

AUSTRIA

HUNGARY

YUGOSLAVIA

ROMANIA

U.S.S.R.

ITALY

SWITZERLAND

LIECHTENSTEIN

Beskids

Carpathians

Sudeten Mts.

Erzgebirge

Bohemian Forest

A L P S

VLTAVA

MORAVA

HRON

TISZA

TISZA

DANUBE

DANUBE

DANUBE

INN

DRAU

DRAVA

LAKE BALATON

LAKE OF CONSTANCE

Kosice

Gerlachovka
8,707 ft.
(2654 m.)

Ostrava

Olomouc

Brno

Hradec
Kralove

Liberec

Usti nad
Labem

⊕ PRAGUE

Plzen

Ceske
Budejovice

Linz

Salzburg

Innsbruck

Grossglockner
12,457 ft.
(3797 m.)

Klagenfurt

Graz

Leoben

⊛ VIENNA

Wiener-
Neustadt

Bratislava ⊚

Szombathely

Gyor

⊕ BUDAPEST

Miskolc

Debrecen

Bekescsaba

Szeged

Kecskemet

Pecs

20°

20°

16°

16°

12°

48°

48°

Longitude East of Greenwich

5,000 m. 16,404 ft.	2,000 m. 6,562 ft.	1,000 m. 3,281 ft.	500 m. 1,640 ft.	200 m. 656 ft.	100 m. 328 ft.	Sea Level	Below

AUSTRIA,
CZECHOSLOVAKIA
AND HUNGARY

100 MI.
75
50
25
0

100 KM.
75
50
25
0

© C.S. Hammond & Co., Maplewood, N.J. 12°

50

THE BALKANS

CZECHOSLOVAKIA

100 m. 200 m. 500 m. 1,000 m. 2,000 m. 5,000 m.
Below Sea 328 ft. 656 ft. 1,640 ft. 3,281 ft. 6,562 ft. 16,404 ft.
Level

POLAND

AUSTRIA

UNION OF SOVIET
SOCIALIST REPUBLICS

HUNGARY

Ljubljana
DRAVA
Zagreb
Rijeka
SAVA
Subotica
DANUBE
Novi Sad
TISZA

Oradea
Arad
Timisoara
Belgrade

Cluj-Napoca
MURES
ROMANIA
Carpathians
Iasi
PRUT
TISZA

Transylvanian
Alps
Brasov
Ploiesti
Galati

Y U G O S L A V I A

Dinaric Alps

Sarajevo

Split

ADRIATIC
SEA

MORAVA

DRIN

Shkoder

Tirane

ALBANIA

Vlore

ITALY

Nis
Skopje
VARDAR

Craiova
OLT
Bucharest
DANUBE
Constanta
Ruse

Balkan Mts.
Sofia
Pleven
Varna
BLACK
SEA
BULGARIA
Burgas
Rhodope Mts.
Plovdiv
MARITSA

G R E E C E

Salonika
Kavalla

PINDUS MTS.

Olympus
9,570 ft.
(2917 m.)

Corfu

Larisa

40°

I O N I A N
SEA

Sicily

Patras

Peloponnesos

Piraeus Athens

AEGEAN SEA

Lesbos

Euboea Chios

CYCLADES

TURKEY

40°

Rhodes

Crete
Candia

M E D I T E R R A N E A N   S E A

0   50   100   150   200 MI.

0   50 100 150 200 KM.

© C.S. Hammond & Co., Maplewood, N.J.   20°   Longitude East of Greenwich

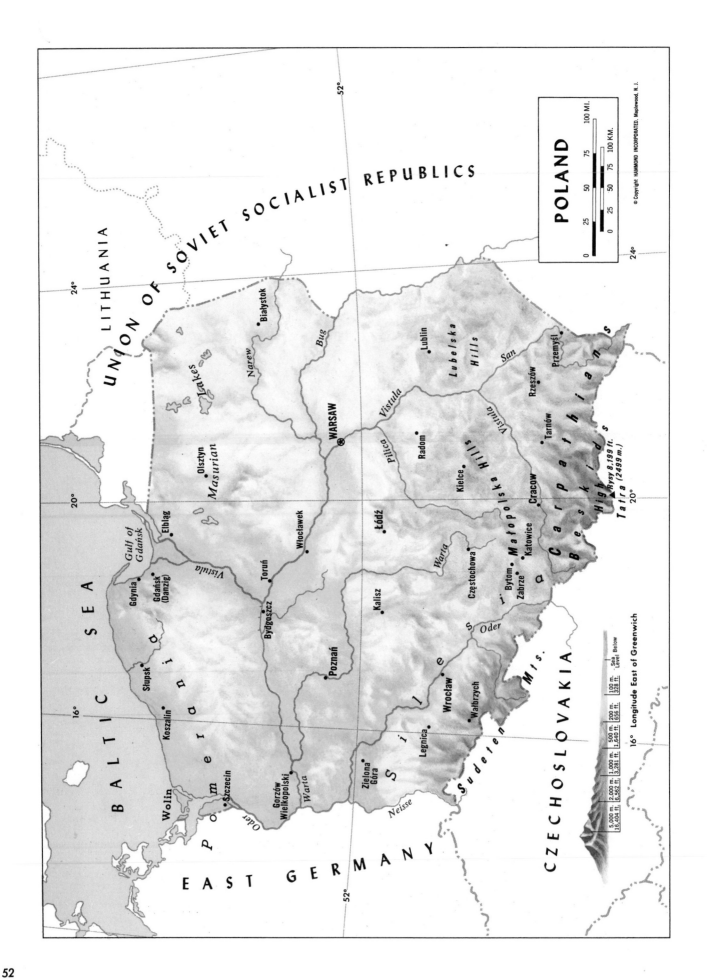

LITHUANIA

UNION OF SOVIET SOCIALIST REPUBLICS

POLAND

© Copyright HAMMOND INCORPORATED, Maplewood, N. J.

100 MI.
100 KM.

Białystok

Narew

Bug

Lublin

Lubelska Hills

San

Przemyśl

Rzeszów

Vistula

WARSAW

Vistula

Tarnów

Carpathians

Pilica

Radom

Kielce

Małopolska Hills

Cracow

Rysy 8,199 ft.
(2499 m.)
Tatra

High Beskids

Olsztyn

Masurian

Lakes

Włocławek

Łódź

Warta

Gulf of Gdańsk

Elbląg

Toruń

Bydgoszcz

Warta

Częstochowa

Bytom
Zabrze
Katowice

Silesia

Oder

Kalisz

Poznań

Gdynia
Gdańsk
(Danzig)

Vistula

BALTIC SEA

Słupsk

Koszalin

Pomerania

Wrocław

Wałbrzych

Sudeten Mts.

Legnica

Zielona Góra

Neisse

Wolin
Szczecin

Gorzów
Wielkopolski

Warta

Oder

CZECHOSLOVAKIA

16° Longitude East of Greenwich

5,000 m. 2,000 m. 1,000 m. 500 m. 200 m. 100 m. Sea
16,404 ft. 6,562 ft. 3,281 ft. 1,640 ft. 656 ft. 328 ft. Level Below

EAST GERMANY

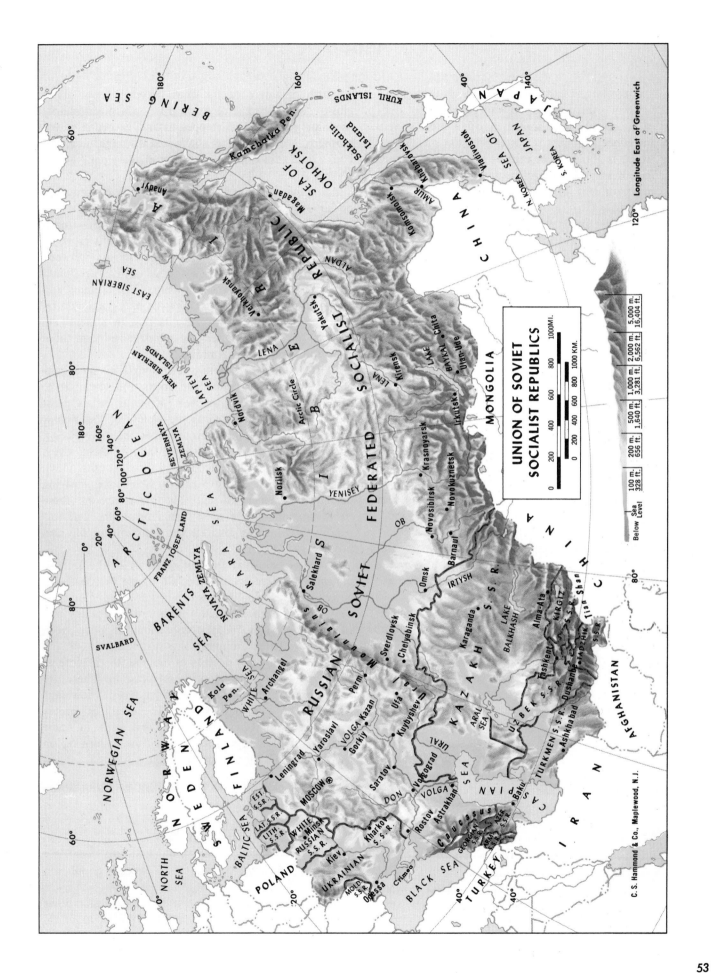

UNION OF SOVIET SOCIALIST REPUBLICS

BERING SEA

Kamchatka Pen

Anadyr

SEA OF OKHOTSK

KURIL ISLANDS

Sakhalin Island

Magadan

Khabarovsk

AMUR

Komsomolsk

Vladivostok

JAPAN

SEA OF JAPAN

N. KOREA

S. KOREA

CHINA

Verkhoyansk

ALDAN

Yakutsk

LENA

RUSSIAN SOVIET FEDERATED SOCIALIST REPUBLIC

Kirensk

Chita

LAKE BAYKAL

Ulan-Ude

Irkutsk

MONGOLIA

Longitude East of Greenwich

120°

EAST SIBERIAN SEA

NEW SIBERIAN ISLANDS

LAPTEV SEA

Nordvik

Arctic Circle

LENA

Krasnoyarsk

Novosibirsk

Novokuznetsk

40°

140°

80°

SEVERNAYA ZEMLYA

Norilsk

YENISEI

OB

Barnaul

CHINA

ARCTIC OCEAN

FRANZ JOSEF LAND

NOVAYA ZEMLYA

KARA SEA

Salekhard

Omsk

IRTYSH

Karaganda

KAZAKH S.S.R.

LAKE BALKHASH

Alma-Ata

KIRGIZ S.S.R.

Tian Shan

80°

SVALBARD

BARENTS SEA

OB

Ob

Sverdlovsk

Chelyabinsk

Ural

ARAL SEA

Tashkent

UZBEK S.S.R.

Dushanbe TADZHIK S.S.R.

AFGHANISTAN

NORWEGIAN SEA

WHITE SEA

Archangel

Kola Pen.

Perm

Kazan

Ufa

Kuybyshev

URAL

TURKMEN S.S.R.

Ashkhabad

IRAN

NORWAY

SWEDEN

FINLAND

Leningrad

Yaroslavl

VOLGA

Gorkiy

Saratov

DON

Volgograd

VOLGA

Astrakhan

CASPIAN SEA

Baku

BALTIC SEA

EST. S.S.R.

LAT. S.S.R.

LITH. S.S.R.

MOSCOW

WHITE RUSSIAN S.S.R.

Minsk

Kharkov

UKRAINIAN S.S.R.

Kiev

Rostov

Caucasus

GEORGIAN S.S.R.

ARM. S.S.R. AZER. S.S.R.

NORTH SEA

POLAND

MOLD. S.S.R.

Odessa

Crimea

BLACK SEA

TURKEY

60°

80°

100°

120°

160°

0°

20°

40°

60°

20°

40°

60°

C. S. Hammond & Co., Maplewood, N.J.

UNION OF SOVIET SOCIALIST REPUBLICS

1000 MI.

800

1000 KM.

600

400

200

0

5,000 m. 16,404 ft.

2,000 m. 6,562 ft.

1,000 m. 3,281 ft.

500 m. 1,640 ft.

200 m. 656 ft.

100 m. 328 ft.

Below Sea Level

ASIA

Asia is the largest continent on earth. It extends almost halfway around the world and covers about one-third of the world's land area. It also has more people than any other continent. Over two billion people live here, which is about 60 percent of the world's population. Asia has more kinds of people and cultures than any other continent. In every way, it is the most varied of continents.

Look at the rainfall map of Asia and find the areas of heavy rainfall. These areas are the continent's most heavily populated places. You may wonder why, with so much land, people crowd into such a small part of Asia. Part of the answer lies in the continent's great size and the way the mountains extend across it.

If you look north of Pakistan, you will see mountains where Afghanistan, the Soviet Union, China, and India meet. These mountains are the Pamir, and they form a knot of mountains which are sometimes called the "roof of the world." From this center, mountains spiral out in different directions, like the spokes of a wheel. They run westward into southern Europe. They stretch southeastward from the Pamir to form the highest mountains in the world, the Himalayas. The Himalayas' highest point, and the highest point on earth, is Mount Everest on the Nepal-China border. The mountains continue south in long lines of deep, forested ravines and continue as a string of islands offshore. The Himalayas and other mountains block the winds that blow north from the oceans and prevent these winds from reaching farther inland. The mountains also stop the cold winds in the north from reaching India. Because of these conditions the center of Asia is very dry and southern Asia is very wet.

From the Pamir knot, mountains run northeastward across Asia. Between the ranges are high plateaus and basins. North of the Himalayas is Tibet, the highest plateau in the world. It can support only a few people. These high, flat areas are not only cold and dry, they are among the most isolated places on earth. To the north of Tibet, between the Tian Shan, Kunlun, and other mountains, you will see lower areas, or basins. They are deserts. The dry land extends northeast through southern Mongolia. The Gobi, one of the world's great deserts, is found here. The few people who have settled in these areas live mostly on oases.

Dry mountainous lands continue southwestward from the Pamir through Pakistan and Afghanistan to merge with the dry plateaus of Iran, Turkey, and the Arabian peninsula. Almost all of southwestern Asia up to about 50° latitude is dry except for part of the land between the Tigris and Euphrates rivers. This region has some of the world's largest petroleum deposits.

North of this area the land becomes lower. It is mostly steppes—areas of short grass, which are mainly used for grazing. The steppes extend eastward across northern Mongolia, arc southward through northern China, and turn west through part of the Huang He or Yellow River, valley.

All of Asia north of the mountains is a continuation of the Great European Plain, and it sinks slowly to the Arctic Ocean. The northernmost area is *tundra*—frozen flatland on which only a few low plants will grow. A zone of pine forests and swamps, called *taiga*, is between the tundra and steppes. Other plains of Asia are found in northern India and eastern China. These plains and the valleys of Southeast Asia are the major agricultural regions of Asia. Most of Asia is rich in mineral resources, but its nations are less industrialized than those in Europe and North America.

Most of the great rivers of Asia begin in the mountains and flow over cliffs and rocks and lowlands to empty sluggishly into the sea. Most of Asia's great civilizations were built along the valleys of the Yellow River, Yangtze, Brahmaputra-Ganges, Indus, Mekong, Irrawaddy, and Salween rivers. Many of these rivers carry soil, which they deposit at their mouths. Also, many of them regularly overflow their banks, leaving behind fresh layers of soil. The plains around these rivers are among the most fertile on earth. Unfortunately, this flooding also causes great loss of life and property.

Most of peninsular India is made up of the Deccan plateau. The Deccan and the hills along the coast are covered with tropical forests.

Asia is fringed by many important peninsulas and islands on which independent countries have been established. There are many bays and seas.

Covering so many degrees of latitude, the climate of Asia would naturally show great variation. There are great extremes of cold and heat in the Russian lowlands (Siberia) and northern China. The south is largely tropical. The heaviest rainfall anywhere is in some localities of southeastern Asia. All of the eastern region has enough rainfall for agriculture.

---

1. What is meant by the term "Eurasia"?
2. List six island countries of Asia.
3. What percentage of the world's land area does Asia occupy? What percentage of the world's population lives in Asia?
4. Asia has many great rivers. Name one that flows north, one that flows east, and one that flows south.

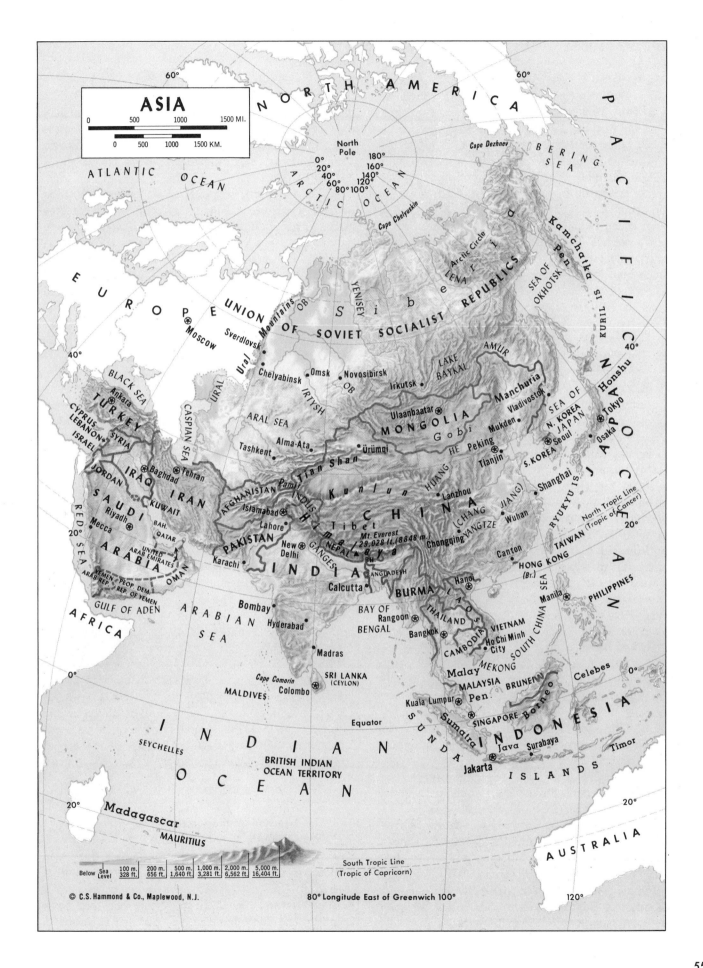

ASIA

0   500   1000   1500 MI.

0   500   1000   1500 KM.

ATLANTIC   OCEAN

NORTH AMERICA

PACIFIC

BERING SEA

Cape Dezhnev

North Pole
0°
20°
40°
60°
80° 100°
120°
140°
160°
180°

ARCTIC OCEAN

Cape Chelyuskin

Arctic Circle

Kamchatka Pen.

SEA OF OKHOTSK

KURIL IS.

SIBERIA

LENA

EUROPE

UNION OF SOVIET SOCIALIST REPUBLICS

Siberia

YENISEY

Moscow

Sverdlovsk

Ural Mountains

OB

AMUR

LAKE BAYKAL

SEA OF JAPAN

Honshu

Tokyo

JAPAN

40°

40°

URAL

Chelyabinsk

Omsk

Novosibirsk

OB

Irkutsk

Vladivostok

Manchuria

Osaka

BLACK SEA

Ankara

TURKEY

CYPRUS
LEBANON
ISRAEL
SYRIA

Ulaanbaatar

MONGOLIA

Gobi

Mukden

N. KOREA

Peking

Seoul

S. KOREA

CASPIAN SEA

ARAL SEA

IRTYSH

Alma-Ata

Ürümqi

HE

Tianjin

Tashkent

Tian Shan

Shanghai

RYUKYU IS.

JORDAN

Baghdad

Tehran

IRAQ

IRAN

AFGHANISTAN

Pamir

Kunlun

HUANG

Lanzhou

ICHANG

JIANG

Wuhan

North Tropic Line
(Tropic of Cancer)

20°

SAUDI

KUWAIT

Riyadh

BAH.

QATAR

Islamabad

INDUS

Tibet

CHINA

Chongqing

YANGTZE

Canton

TAIWAN

20°

Mecca

UNITED ARAB EMIRATES

PAKISTAN

Lahore

New Delhi

Mt. Everest
29,028 ft.(8848 m.)

Himalaya

Nepal

Bhutan

HONG KONG
(Br.)

RED SEA

ARABIA

OMAN

Karachi

GANGES

INDIA

BANGLADESH

Hanoi

YEMEN PEOP. DEM.
ARAB REP. REP. OF YEMEN

Calcutta

BURMA

LAOS

Manila

PHILIPPINES

GULF OF ADEN

ARABIAN SEA

Bombay

BAY OF BENGAL

Rangoon

THAILAND

VIETNAM

SOUTH CHINA SEA

AFRICA

Hyderabad

Bangkok

CAMBODIA

Ho Chi Minh City

Madras

MEKONG

Malay

Celebes

0°

Cape Comorin

SRI LANKA
(CEYLON)

MALAYSIA

BRUNEI

Borneo

0°

MALDIVES

Colombo

Kuala Lumpur

Pen.

SEYCHELLES

INDIAN

Equator

Sumatra

SINGAPORE

INDONESIA

BRITISH INDIAN OCEAN TERRITORY

OCEAN

SUNDA

Java

Surabaya

Timor

ISLANDS

Jakarta

20°

Madagascar

MAURITIUS

20°

AUSTRALIA

Below Sea Level | 100 m. 328 ft. | 200 m. 656 ft. | 500 m. 1,640 ft. | 1,000 m. 3,281 ft. | 2,000 m. 6,562 ft. | 5,000 m. 16,404 ft.

South Tropic Line
(Tropic of Capricorn)

© C.S. Hammond & Co., Maplewood, N.J.

80° Longitude East of Greenwich 100°

120°

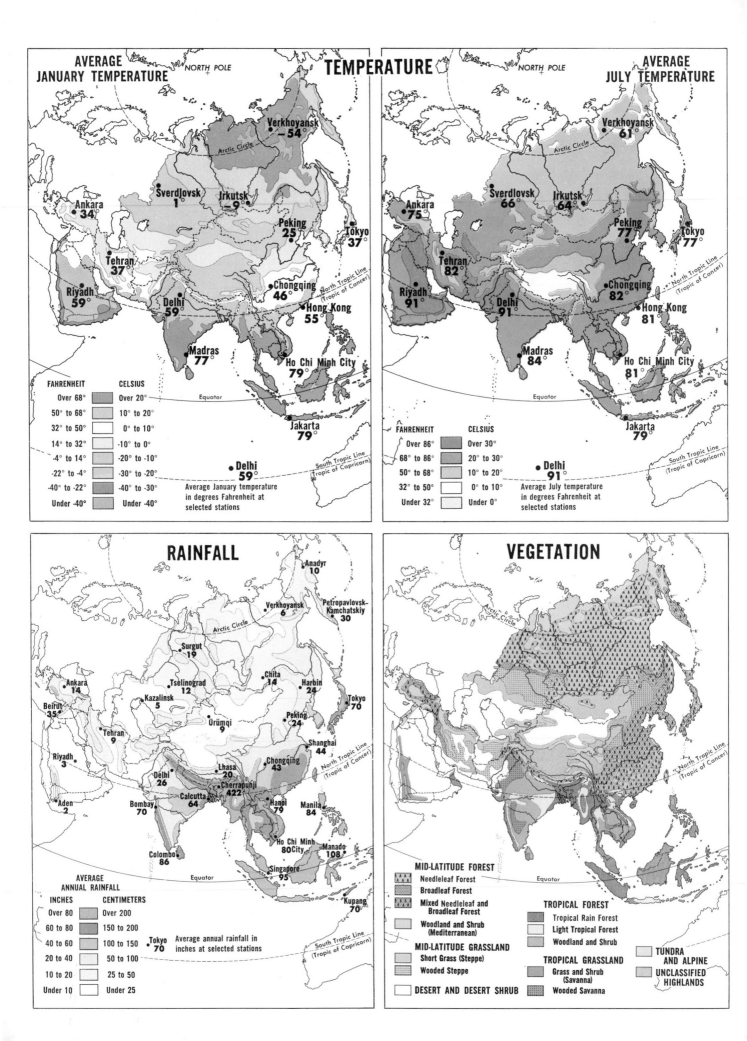

TEMPERATURE

AVERAGE JANUARY TEMPERATURE

NORTH POLE

Verkhoyansk −54

Sverdlovsk 1

Irkutsk −9

Ankara 34

Peking 25

Tokyo 37

Tehran 37

Chongqing 46

Riyadh 59

Delhi 59

Hong Kong 55

Madras 77

Ho Chi Minh City 79

Jakarta 79

Arctic Circle

North Tropic Line (Tropic of Cancer)

Equator

South Tropic Line (Tropic of Capricorn)

FAHRENHEIT	CELSIUS
Over 68°	Over 20°
50° to 68°	10° to 20°
32° to 50°	0° to 10°
14° to 32°	-10° to 0°
-4° to 14°	-20° to -10°
-22° to -4°	-30° to -20°
-40° to -22°	-40° to -30°
Under -40°	Under -40°

Delhi 59°

Average January temperature in degrees Fahrenheit at selected stations

AVERAGE JULY TEMPERATURE

NORTH POLE

Verkhoyansk 61

Sverdlovsk 66

Irkutsk 64

Ankara 75

Peking 77

Tokyo 77

Tehran 82

Chongqing 82

Riyadh 91

Delhi 91

Hong Kong 81

Madras 84

Ho Chi Minh City 81

Jakarta 79

Arctic Circle

North Tropic Line (Tropic of Cancer)

Equator

South Tropic Line (Tropic of Capricorn)

FAHRENHEIT	CELSIUS
Over 86°	Over 30°
68° to 86°	20° to 30°
50° to 68°	10° to 20°
32° to 50°	0° to 10°
Under 32°	Under 0°

Delhi 91°

Average July temperature in degrees Fahrenheit at selected stations

RAINFALL

Anadyr 10

Verkhoyansk 6

Petropavlovsk-Kamchatskiy 30

Surgut 19

Chita 14

Harbin 24

Tselinograd 12

Tokyo 70

Kazalinsk 5

Peking 24

Ürümqi 9

Shanghai 44

Ankara 14

Beirut 35

Tehran 9

Chongqing 43

Riyadh 3

Lhasa 20

Cherrapunji 422

Aden 2

Delhi 26

Calcutta 64

Hanoi 79

Manila 84

Bombay 70

Ho Chi Minh City 80

Manado 108

Colombo 86

Singapore 95

Kupang 70

Arctic Circle

North Tropic Line (Tropic of Cancer)

Equator

South Tropic Line (Tropic of Capricorn)

AVERAGE ANNUAL RAINFALL

INCHES	CENTIMETERS
Over 80	Over 200
60 to 80	150 to 200
40 to 60	100 to 150
20 to 40	50 to 100
10 to 20	25 to 50
Under 10	Under 25

Tokyo 70 — Average annual rainfall in inches at selected stations

VEGETATION

Arctic Circle

North Tropic Line (Tropic of Cancer)

Equator

MID-LATITUDE FOREST
- Needleleaf Forest
- Broadleaf Forest
- Mixed Needleleaf and Broadleaf Forest
- Woodland and Shrub (Mediterranean)

MID-LATITUDE GRASSLAND
- Short Grass (Steppe)
- Wooded Steppe

DESERT AND DESERT SHRUB

TROPICAL FOREST
- Tropical Rain Forest
- Light Tropical Forest
- Woodland and Shrub

TROPICAL GRASSLAND
- Grass and Shrub (Savanna)
- Wooded Savanna

TUNDRA AND ALPINE

UNCLASSIFIED HIGHLANDS

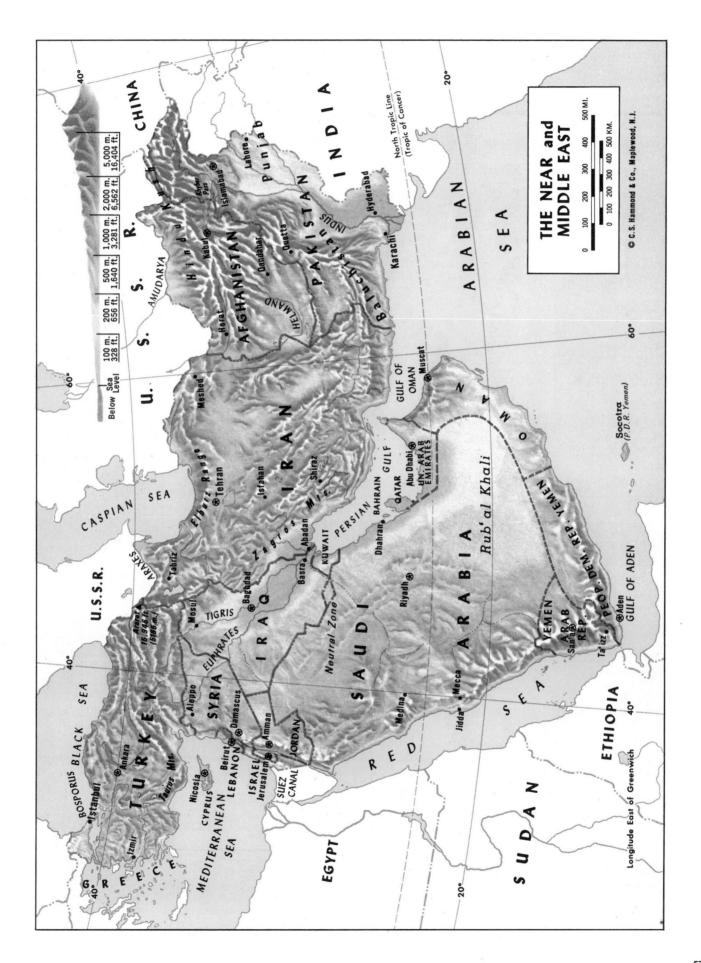

THE NEAR and MIDDLE EAST

500 MI.
0   100 200 300 400
0   100 200 300 400 500 KM.

© C. S. Hammond & Co., Maplewood, N.J.

CHINA

U. S. S. R.

INDIA

Punjab
Lahore
Islamabad
Khyber Pass
Hindu Kush
Kabul
AFGHANISTAN
Qandahar
Quetta
PAKISTAN
Baluchistan
INDUS
Hyderabad
Karachi

Herat
HELMAND
AMUDARYA

Meshed

Elburz Range
Tehran
Isfahan
IRAN
Shiraz
Zagros Mts.

CASPIAN SEA

Tabriz
ARAKES

Ararat
16,946 ft.
(5165 m.)

U.S.S.R.

Mosul
TIGRIS
Bagdad
EUPHRATES
IRAQ
Basra
Abadan
KUWAIT

Neutral Zone

SAUDI

Riyadh

ARABIA

Rub'al Khali

North Tropic Line
(Tropic of Cancer)

20°

ARABIAN

SEA

60°

GULF OF OMAN
Muscat
O M A N

Abu Dhabi
UN-ARAB EMIRATES
QATAR
BAHRAIN
PERSIAN GULF
Dhahran

Socotra
(P. D. R. Yemen)

YEMEN PEOP. DEM. REP.

YEMEN ARAB REP.
San'a
Ta'izz
Aden
GULF OF ADEN

40°

Mecca
Medina
Jidda

RED SEA

ETHIOPIA

SUDAN

EGYPT

SUEZ CANAL

Amman
JORDAN
Damascus
SYRIA
Aleppo
Beirut
LEBANON
ISRAEL
Jerusalem
Nicosia
CYPRUS

MEDITERRANEAN SEA

Ankara
TURKEY
Taurus Mts.
Istanbul
Izmir
BOSPORUS
BLACK SEA

GREECE

Longitude East of Greenwich

40°

60°

5,000 m.
16,404 ft.

2,000 m.
6,562 ft.

1,000 m.
3,281 ft.

500 m.
1,640 ft.

200 m.
656 ft.

100 m.
328 ft.

Sea Level

Below Sea Level

57

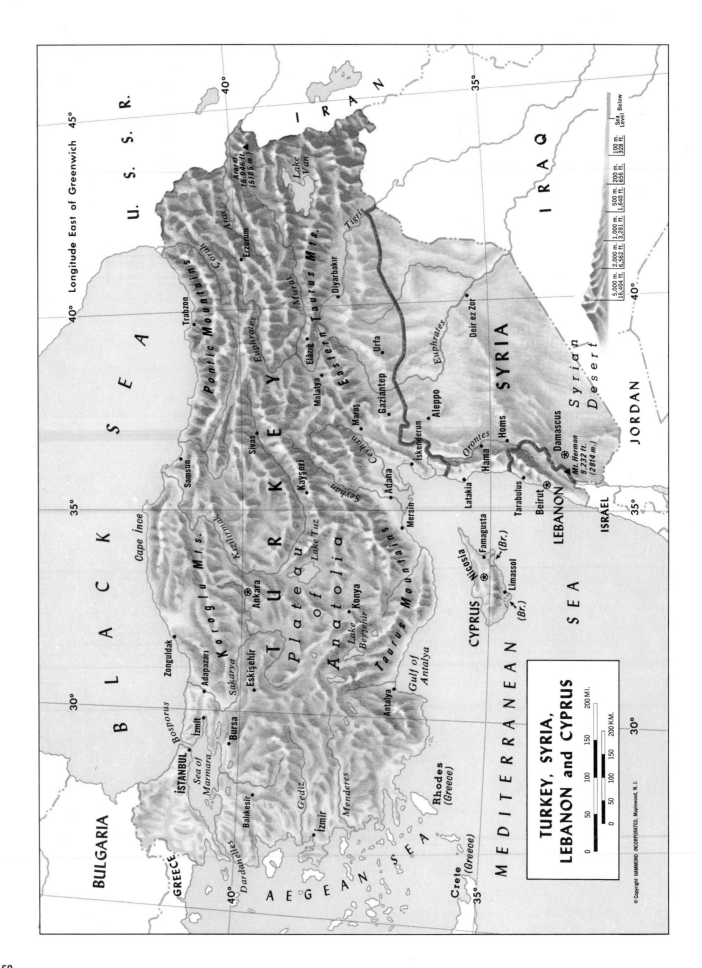

TURKEY, SYRIA, LEBANON and CYPRUS

© Copyright HAMMOND INCORPORATED, Maplewood, N.J.

200 MI.
200 KM.

BULGARIA

GREECE

BLACK SEA

Cape İnce

İSTANBUL
Sea of Marmara
Bosporus
İzmit
Bursa
Adapazarı
Zonguldak
Sakarya
Eskişehir
Balıkesir
Dardanelles
Gediz
İzmir
Menderes
Rhodes (Greece)
Crete (Greece)

AEGEAN SEA

MEDITERRANEAN SEA

Köroğlu Mts.
Ankara
Kızılırmak
Lake Tuz
Plateau of Anatolia
Konya
Lake Beyşehir
Antalya
Gulf of Antalya
Taurus Mountains

T U R K E Y

Eskişehir
Sivas
Kayseri
Seyhan
Ceyhan
Mersin
Adana
İskenderun

Trabzon
Pontic Mountains
Çoruh
Aras
Erzurum
Ararat 16,946 ft. (5165 m.)
Lake Van
Murat
Euphrates
Elazığ
Malatya
Maraş
Gaziantep
Eastern Taurus Mts.
Diyarbakır
Tigris
Urfa
Euphrates
Aleppo
Deir ez Zor

Samsun

U. S. S. R.

Longitude East of Greenwich

I R A N

I R A Q

S Y R I A
Syrian Desert
Hama
Homs
Orontes
Damascus
Mt. Hermon 9,232 ft. (2814 m.)

Latakia
Tarabulus
Beirut
LEBANON
ISRAEL
JORDAN

Nicosia
Famagusta (Br.)
Limassol (Br.)
CYPRUS

45°
40°
40°
35°
40°
40°
35°
35°
30°
30°
35°
30°

5,000 m. | 2,000 m. | 1,000 m. | 500 m. | 200 m. | 100 m. | Sea Level | Below
16,404 ft. | 6,562 ft. | 3,281 ft. | 1,640 ft. | 656 ft. | 328 ft. | |

58

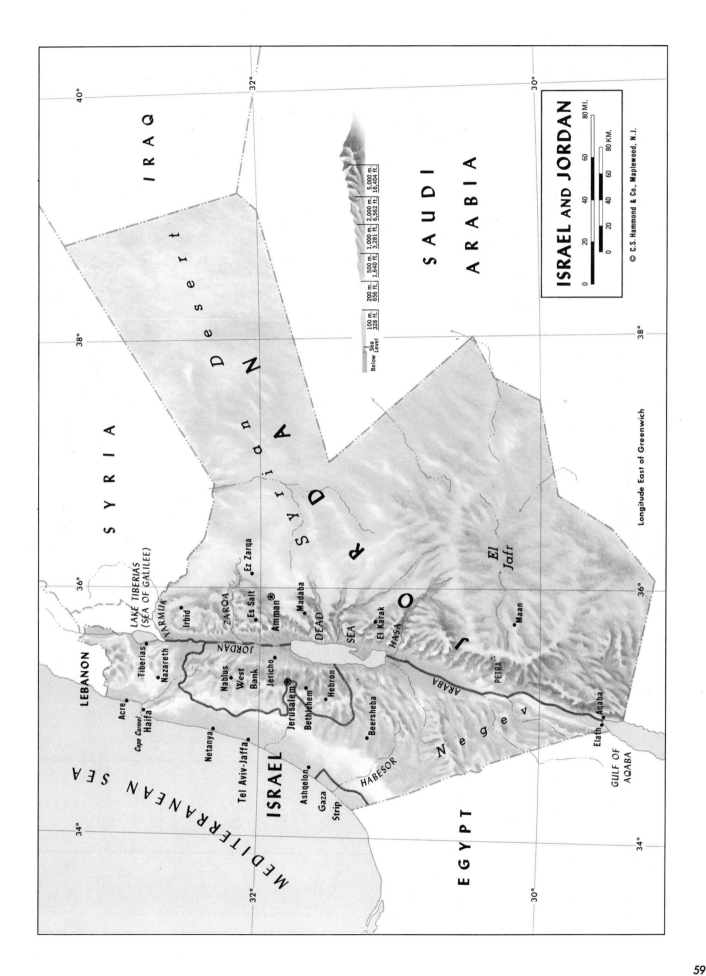

ISRAEL AND JORDAN

© C.S. Hammond & Co., Maplewood, N.J.

100 m. 200 m. 500 m. 1,000 m. 2,000 m. 5,000 m.
328 ft. 656 ft. 1,640 ft. 3,281 ft. 6,562 ft. 16,404 ft.

Sea Level
Below Sea Level

IRAQ

SYRIA

SAUDI ARABIA

Jordan Desert

JORDAN

El Jafr

Maan

Amman
Es Salt
ZARQA
Ez Zarqa
Madaba
Irbid
YARMUK
LAKE TIBERIAS
(SEA OF GALILEE)
Tiberias
Nazareth

DEAD SEA
El Karak
HASA

PETRA

ARABA

LEBANON
Acre
Cape Carmel
Haifa
Netanya
Tel Aviv-Jaffa
Ashqelon
Gaza Strip

Nablus
West Bank
Jericho
Jerusalem
Bethlehem
Hebron
Beersheba

ISRAEL

HABESOR

Negev

MEDITERRANEAN SEA

EGYPT

Elath Aqaba

GULF OF AQABA

Longitude East of Greenwich

40°

38°

36°

34°

32°

30°

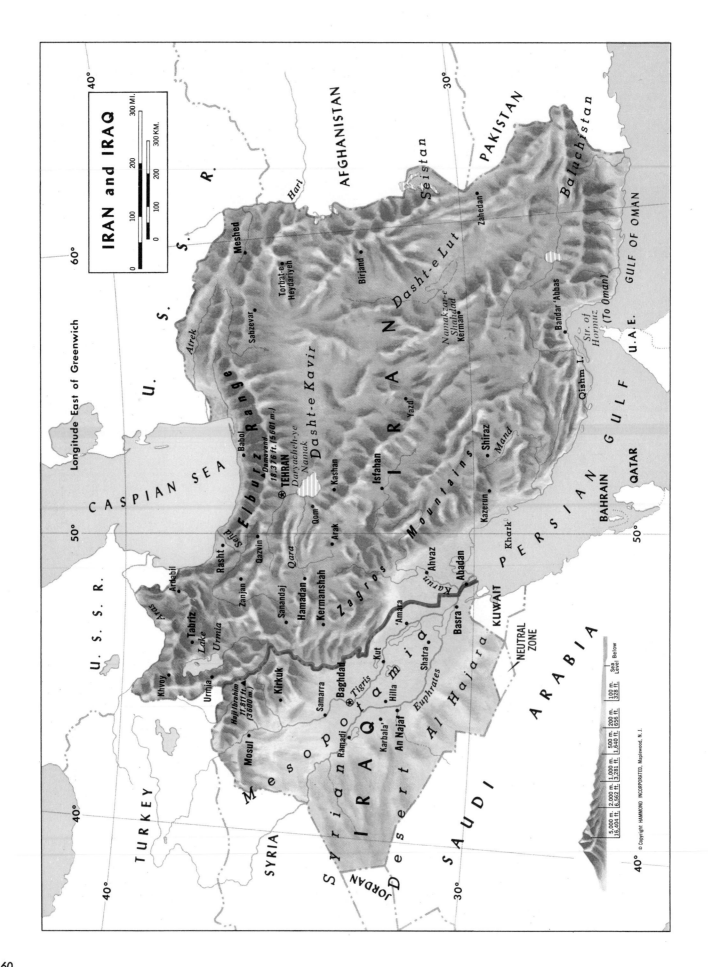

IRAN and IRAQ

300 MI.

300 KM.

Longitude East of Greenwich

U. S. S. R.

TURKEY

SYRIA

JORDAN

SAUDI   ARABIA

Mosul

Haji Ibrahim
11,811 ft.
(3600 m.)

Khvoy

Urmia

Tabriz

Lake
Urmia

Ardabil

Aras

Zanjan

Qazvin

Rasht

Sefid

Qara

Kirkuk

Samarra

Baghdad

Tigris

Kut

Ramadi

Karbala'

An Najaf

Hilla

Euphrates

Shatra

'Amara

Basra

KUWAIT

NEUTRAL
ZONE

Mesopotamia

Syrian   Desert

Al Hajara

IRAQ

CASPIAN SEA

Babol

Damavand
18,376 ft. (5601 m.)

Elburz Range

TEHRAN

Daryacheh-ye
Namak

Qom

Arak

Kashan

Dasht-e Kavir

Isfahan

Yazd

Sanandaj

Hamadan

Kermanshah

Zagros

Kazerun

Shiraz

Mand

Mountains

Ahvaz

Ahadan

Karun

Khark

P

PERSIAN

GULF

BAHRAIN

QATAR

U.A.E.

Meshed

Hari

Sabzevar

Torbat-e
Heydariyeh

Birjand

Dasht-e Lut

Namakzar-e
Shahdad

Kerman

I R A N

Zahedan

Seistan

AFGHANISTAN

PAKISTAN

Baluchistan

Bandar Abbas

Qishm I.

Sir of
Hormuz.
(To Oman)

GULF OF OMAN

40°

60°

50°

40°

30°

30°

40°

50°

30°

U. S. S. R.

5,000 m. 2,000 m. 1,000 m. 500 m. 200 m. 100 m. Sea   Below
16,404 ft. 6,562 ft. 3,281 ft. 1,640 ft. 656 ft. 328 ft. Level

© Copyright HAMMOND INCORPORATED, Maplewood, N. J.

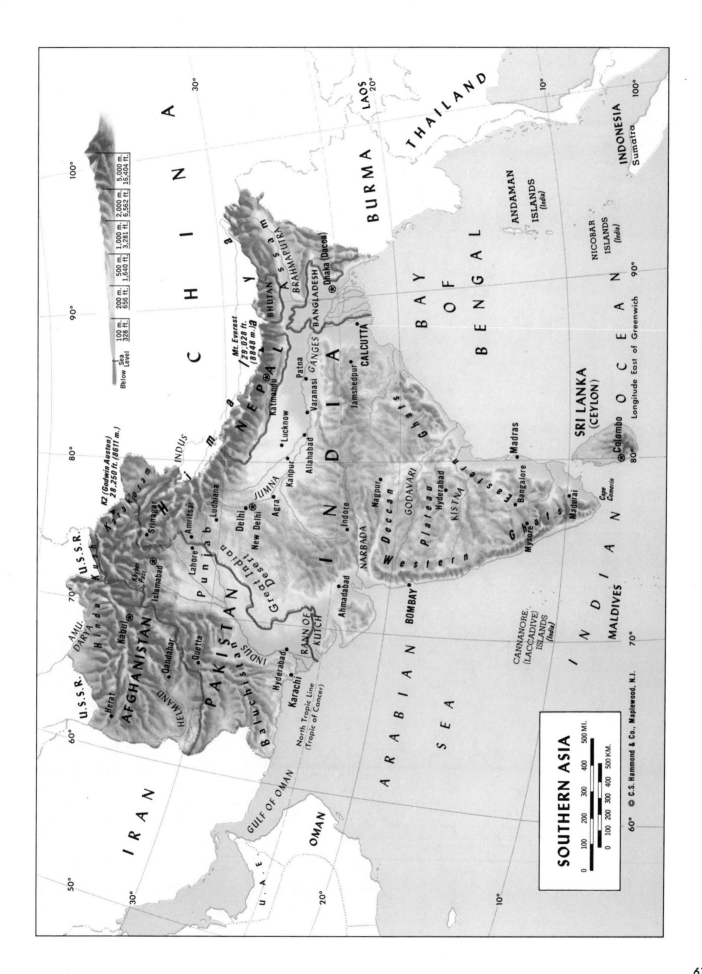

CHINA

30°

100°

LAOS 20°

THAILAND

BURMA

INDONESIA
Sumatra

100°

10°

5,000 m. 16,404 ft.
2,000 m. 6,562 ft.
1,000 m. 3,281 ft.
500 m. 1,640 ft.
200 m. 656 ft.
100 m. 328 ft.
Sea Level
Below Level

ANDAMAN
ISLANDS
(India)

NICOBAR
ISLANDS
(India)

90°

Assam
BRAHMAPUTRA

BHUTAN

Dhaka (Dacca)

BANGLADESH

⊕ Dhaka (Dacca)

B A Y

O F

B E N G A L

Mt. Everest 29,028 ft. (8848 m.)▲

Katmandu ⊕

N E P A L

Patna

GANGES

CALCUTTA

Lucknow

Varanasi

Allahabad

Jamshedpur

I N D I A

SRI LANKA
(CEYLON)

O C E A N

Longitude East of Greenwich

80°

K2 (Godwin Austen) 28,250 ft. (8611 m.)

Srinagar

Karakoram

H

i

m

a

l

a

y

a

INDUS

JUMNA

Kanpur

Ghats

Madras

Amritsar

Ludhiana

Punjab

Delhi

Agra

Indore

Nagpur

Deccan

GODAVARI

Plateau

Hyderabad

Eastern

Bangalore

Mysore

Colombo ⊗

Cape Comorin

80°

H
Hindu Kush

U.S.S.R.

Kabul ⊗

New Delhi ⊕

Great Indian Desert

Ahmadabad

NARBADA

Western

KISTNA

Ghats

Madurai

70°

AMU DARYA

Herat

AFGHANISTAN

Qandahar

Quetta

Islamabad ⊗

Lahore

PAKISTAN

Baluchistan

INDUS

HELMAND

Khyber Pass

Hyderabad

RANN OF KUTCH

BOMBAY

CANNANORE (LACCADIVE) ISLANDS (India)

MALDIVES

70°

Karachi

North Tropic Line (Tropic of Cancer)

A R A B I A N

S E A

I N D I A N

60°

IRAN

GULF OF OMAN

U.A.E.

OMAN

20°

10°

SOUTHERN ASIA

0   100   200   300   400   500 MI.

0   100 200 300 400   500 KM.

© C.S. Hammond & Co., Maplewood, N.J.

50°

30°

61

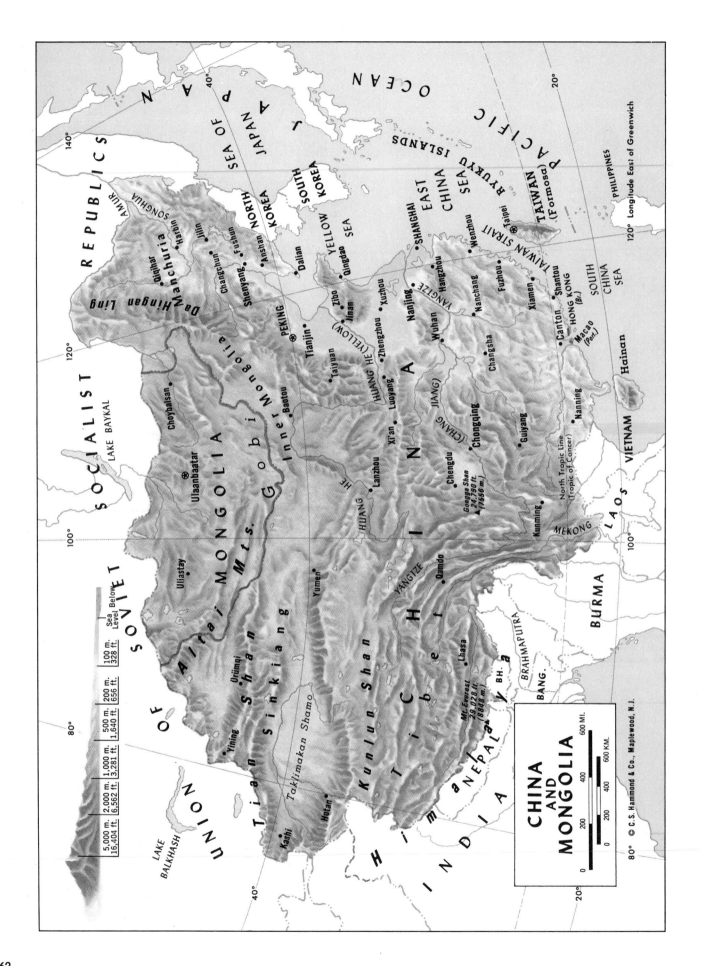

CHINA
AND
MONGOLIA

© C.S. Hammond & Co., Maplewood, N.J.

600 MI.
400
200
0

600 KM.
400
200
0

Sea Level Below | 100 m. 328 ft. | 200 m. 656 ft. | 500 m. 1,640 ft. | 1,000 m. 3,281 ft. | 2,000 m. 6,562 ft. | 5,000 m. 16,404 ft.

PACIFIC OCEAN

JAPAN

SEA OF JAPAN

RYUKYU ISLANDS

EAST CHINA SEA

SOUTH CHINA SEA

TAIWAN (Formosa)
Taipei

PHILIPPINES

120° Longitude East of Greenwich

NORTH KOREA

SOUTH KOREA

YELLOW SEA

Shanghai
Wenzhou
Hangzhou
Nanchang
Fuzhou
Xiamen
Shantou
Canton
HONG KONG (Br.)
Macao (Port.)
Hainan

SOCIALIST REPUBLICS

LAKE BAYKAL

AMUR
SONGHUA
Harbin
Qiqihar
Manchuria
Da Hingan Ling
Jilin
Changchun
Fushun
Anshan
Shenyang
Dalian
Qingdao
Zibo
Jinan
Xuzhou
Zhengzhou
Nanjing
Wuhan
Changsha
Guiyang
Nanning
VIETNAM

PEKING
Tianjin
Taiyuan
Luoyang
HUANG HE (YELLOW)
Xi'an
Lanzhou
Chengdu
Chongqing
Gongga Shan 24,790 ft. (7556 m.)
Kunming
MEKONG
LAOS
BURMA

Choybalsan
Ulaanbaatar
MONGOLIA
Gobi
Inner Mongolia
Baotou
HE
HUANG
Uliastay
Altai Mts.
Yumen
Qamdo
YANGTZE
Ürümqi
Tian Shan
Sinkiang
Taklimakan Shamo
Kunlun Shan
Tibet
Lhasa
Mt. Everest 29,028 ft. (8848 m.)
Himalaya
BH.
BRAHMAPUTRA
BANG.
NEPAL
INDIA

Yining
Hotan
Kashi
LAKE BALKHASH

UNION OF SOVIET

North Tropic Line (Tropic of Cancer)

CHINA

CHANG (JIANG)

62

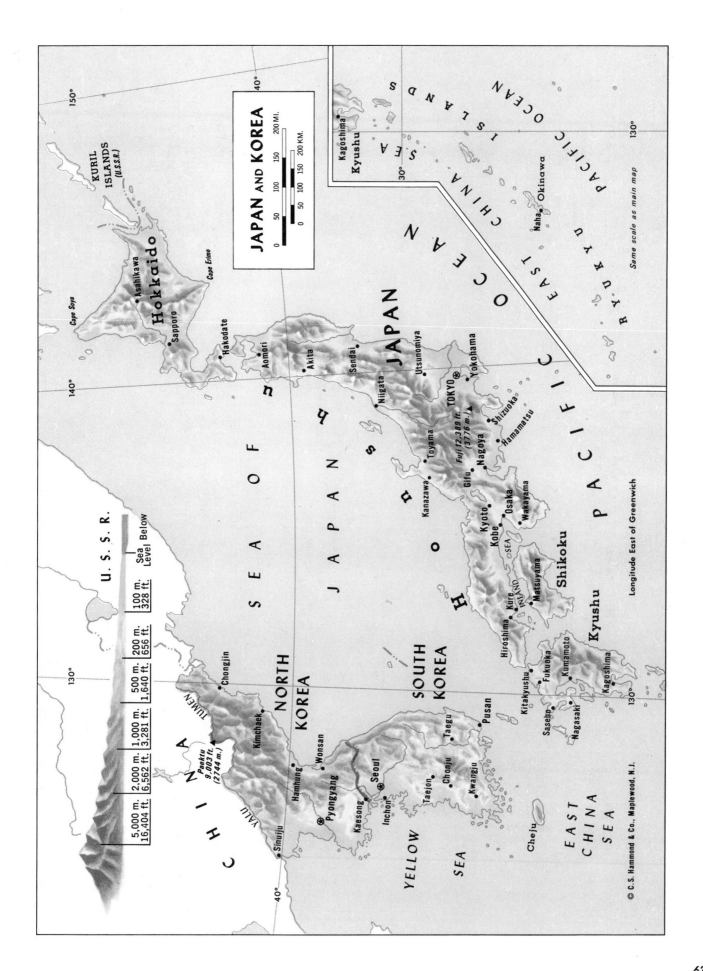

JAPAN AND KOREA

200 MI.

0 50 100 150 200 KM.

Same scale as main map

KURIL ISLANDS *(U.S.S.R.)*

Cape Soya
Asahikawa
Hokkaido
Cape Erimo
Sapporo
Hakodate
Aomori
Akita
Sendai
JAPAN
Niigata
Utsunomiya
TOKYO ⊕
Yokohama
Toyama
Fuji 12,389 ft.
(3776 m.) ▲
Kanazawa
Nagoya
Shizuoka
Gifu
Hamamatsu
Kyoto
Osaka
Kobe
Wakayama
SEA
INLAND
Kure
Matsuyama
Shikoku
Hiroshima
Kyushu
Kitakyushu
Fukuoka
Kumamoto
Sasebo
Kagoshima
Nagasaki

H o n s h u

Kagoshima
Kyushu
Naha • Okinawa

RYUKYU ISLANDS

EAST CHINA SEA

CHINA SEA

PACIFIC OCEAN

PACIFIC

OCEAN

SEA OF JAPAN

S E A O F J A P A N

U.S.S.R.

Sea Level Below
100 m. 328 ft.
200 m. 656 ft.
500 m. 1,640 ft.
1,000 m. 3,281 ft.
2,000 m. 6,562 ft.
5,000 m. 16,404 ft.

Chongjin
Kimchaek
NORTH KOREA
Hamhung
Wonsan
Pyongyang
Paektu 9,003 ft. (2744 m.) ▲
TUMEN
Sinuiju
YALU
CHINA
Kaesong
Seoul ⊕
Inchon
SOUTH KOREA
Taejon
Chonju
Kwangju
Taegu
Pusan
Cheju

YELLOW SEA

EAST CHINA SEA

Longitude East of Greenwich

130°

40°

150°

140°

130°

40°

30°

130°

© C.S. Hammond & Co., Maplewood, N.J.

63

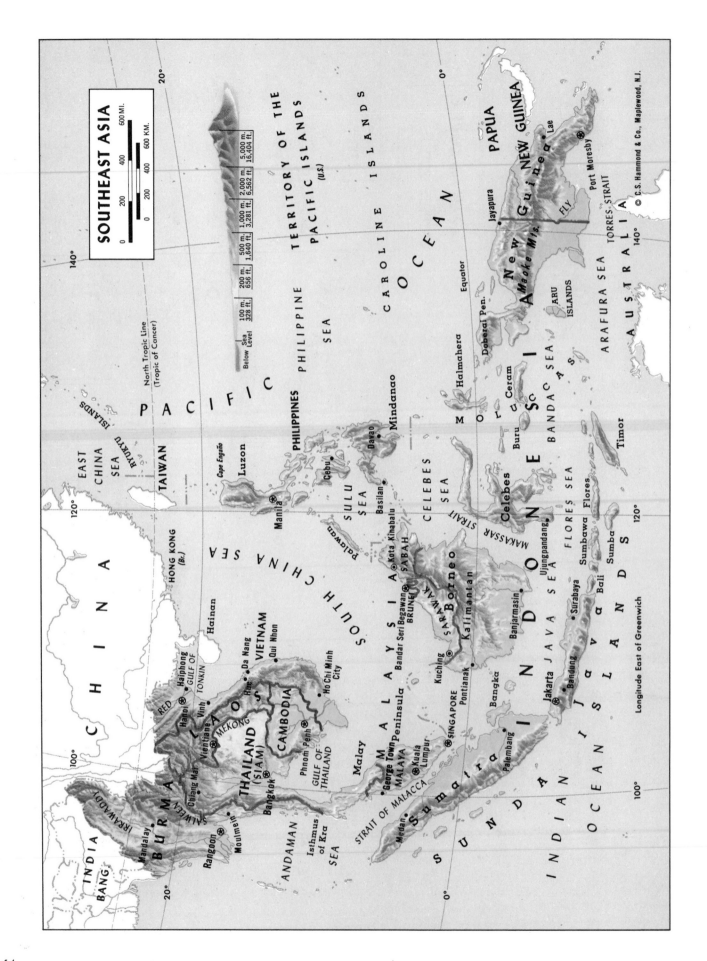

SOUTHEAST ASIA

600 MI.
400
200
0

600 KM.
400
200
0

5,000 m.
16,404 ft.
2,000 m.
6,562 ft.
1,000 m.
3,281 ft.
500 m.
1,640 ft.
200 m.
656 ft.
100 m.
328 ft.
Sea
Level
Below
Sea Level

CHINA

INDIA

BANG.

BURMA

IRRAWADDY

Mandalay

SALWEEN

Moulmein

Rangoon

Chiang Mai

THAILAND
(SIAM)

Bangkok

LAOS

MEKONG

Vientiane

Phnom Penh

CAMBODIA

VIETNAM

RED

Hanoi

Haiphong

Vinh

GULF OF
TONKIN

Da Nang

Rhe

Qui Nhon

Ho Chi Minh
City

Hainan

HONG KONG
(Br.)

EAST
CHINA
SEA

RYUKYU

ISLANDS

TAIWAN

SOUTH CHINA SEA

GULF OF
THAILAND

ANDAMAN
SEA

Isthmus
of Kra

Malay

Peninsula

MALAYA

George Town

Kuala
Lumpur

STRAIT OF MALACCA

Medan

Sumatra

SUNDA

Palembang

Bangka

Jakarta

Bandung

JAVA SEA

Java

Surabaya

Bali

INDIAN

OCEAN

ISLANDS

Sumba

Sumbawa

Flores

FLORES SEA

Timor

BANDA SEA

Ujungpandang

MAKASSAR STRAIT

Celebes

CELEBES
SEA

Kalimantan

Borneo

Banjarmasin

Pontianak

Kuching

SINGAPORE

MALAYSIA

Bandar Seri Begawan

BRUNEI

SARAWAK

SABAH

Kota Kinabalu

SULU
SEA

Palawan

Basilan

Manila

Cebu

Luzon

Cape Engaño

PHILIPPINES

Davao

Mindanao

PHILIPPINE
SEA

PACIFIC

OCEAN

CAROLINE ISLANDS

TERRITORY OF THE
PACIFIC ISLANDS
(U.S.)

Halmahera

Buru

Ceram

M
O
L
U
C
C
A
S

Doberai Pen.

New Guinea

Maoke Mts.

Jayapura

PAPUA NEW GUINEA

PAPUA

Lae

Port Moresby

FLY

TORRES STRAIT

ARU
ISLANDS

ARAFURA SEA

AUSTRALIA

INDONESIA

Equator

North Tropic Line
(Tropic of Cancer)

Longitude East of Greenwich

20°

140°

120°

100°

0°

140°

120°

100°

0°

20°

© C.S. Hammond & Co., Maplewood, N.J.

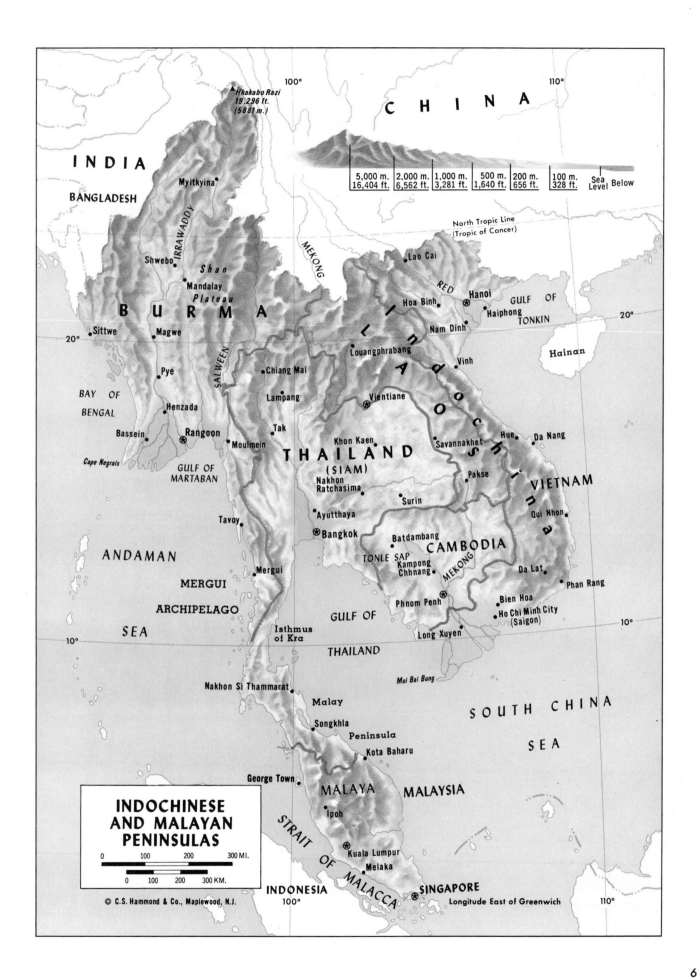

INDIA

BANGLADESH

▲ *Hkakabo Razi*
19,296 ft.
(5881 m.)

100°

CHINA

110°

| 5,000 m. | 2,000 m. | 1,000 m. | 500 m. | 200 m. | 100 m. | Sea | |
| 16,404 ft. | 6,562 ft. | 3,281 ft. | 1,640 ft. | 656 ft. | 328 ft. | Level | Below |

North Tropic Line
(Tropic of Cancer)

Myitkyina•

Shwebo•

IRRAWADDY

Shan
Plateau

MEKONG

Lao Cai•

RED

Hoa Binh• ⊛ Hanoi
Haiphong

GULF OF
TONKIN

20°

BURMA

Mandalay•

Nam Dinh•

•Sittwe

•Magwe

20°

SALWEEN

Louangphrabang•

Vinh•

Hainan

Pye•

Chiang Mai•

Indochina

BAY OF
BENGAL

Lampang•

•Vientiane

Henzada•

⊛Rangoon

Tak•

Bassein•

Moulmein•

THAILAND
(SIAM)

Khon Kaen•

Savannakhet•

Hue• Da Nang•

Cape Negrais

GULF OF
MARTABAN

Nakhon
Ratchasima

Pakse•

VIETNAM

Surin•

Tavoy•

Ayutthaya•

Qui Nhon•

⊛Bangkok

Batdambang•

CAMBODIA

ANDAMAN

TONLE SAP
Kampong
Chhnang•

MEKONG

Da Lat•

MERGUI

Mergui•

Phan Rang•

ARCHIPELAGO

GULF OF
THAILAND

Phnom Penh⊛

Bien Hoa•
•Ho Chi Minh City
(Saigon)

SEA

Isthmus
of Kra

Long Xuyen•

10°

10°

Mui Bai Bung

Nakhon Si Thammarat•

SOUTH CHINA

Malay•

SEA

Songkhla•

Peninsula

Kota Baharu•

George Town•

MALAYA

MALAYSIA

Ipoh•

STRAIT

⊛ Kuala Lumpur
Melaka•

OF

INDONESIA

MALACCA

SINGAPORE•

100°

Longitude East of Greenwich

110°

INDOCHINESE
AND MALAYAN
PENINSULAS

0   100   200   300 MI.

0   100   200   300 KM.

© C.S. Hammond & Co., Maplewood, N.J.

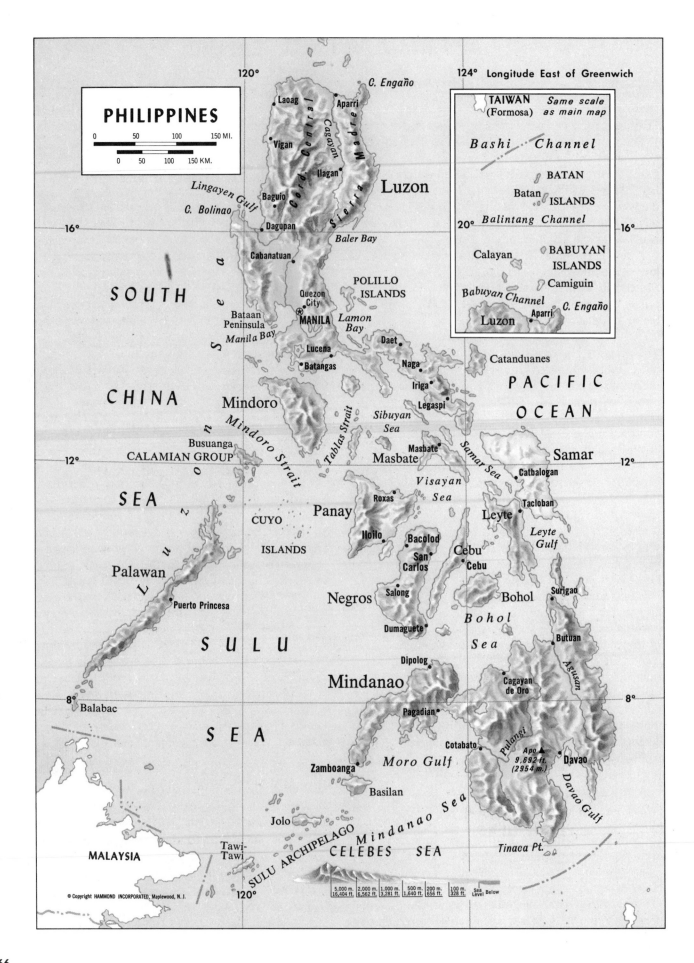

PHILIPPINES

0 50 100 150 MI.

0 50 100 150 KM.

120°   **124°**   Longitude East of Greenwich

C. Engaño

Laoag

Aparri

Cagayan

Cord. Central

Sierra Madre

Vigan

Ilagan

Luzon

Lingayen Gulf

Baguio

C. Bolinao

16°   Dagupan

Baler Bay

Cabanatuan

S O U T H

S e a

POLILLO ISLANDS

Quezon City

Bataan Peninsula

⊛ **MANILA**

Lamon Bay

Manila Bay

Daet

C H I N A

Lucena

Batangas

Naga

Iriga

Catanduanes

Mindoro

Legaspi

P A C I F I C

Sibuyan Sea

O C E A N

Tablas Strait

Mindoro Strait

Busuanga

CALAMIAN GROUP

Masbate

Masbate

Samar Sea

Samar

12°   Catbalogan   **12°**

S E A

Visayan Sea

Roxas

Leyte

Tacloban

L u z o n

CUYO ISLANDS

Panay

Iloilo

Bacolod

San Carlos

Cebu

Cebu

Leyte Gulf

Palawan

Salong

Negros

Bohol

Surigao

Puerto Princesa

Dumaguete

Bohol Sea

Butuan

S U L U

Dipolog

Agusan

Mindanao

Cagayan de Oro

8°   Balabac   **8°**

S E A

Pagadian

Cotabato

Pulangi

Apo ▲ 9,692 ft. (2954 m.)

Davao

Zamboanga

Moro Gulf

Davao Gulf

Basilan

MALAYSIA

Jolo

Tawi-Tawi

SULU ARCHIPELAGO

Mindanao Sea

Tinaca Pt.

C E L E B E S   S E A

© Copyright HAMMOND INCORPORATED, Maplewood, N.J.

120°

5,000 m. 16,404 ft. | 2,000 m. 6,562 ft. | 1,000 m. 3,281 ft. | 500 m. 1,640 ft. | 200 m. 656 ft. | 100 m. 328 ft. | Sea Level | Below

TAIWAN (Formosa)   Same scale as main map

Bashi   Channel

BATAN

Batan

ISLANDS

20°   Balintang   Channel   **16°**

Calayan

BABUYAN ISLANDS

Camiguin

Babuyan Channel

C. Engaño

Luzon

Aparri

AUSTRALIA AND NEW ZEALAND

Australia is the world's smallest continent. It lies entirely below the equator and for that reason is sometimes referred to as the continent "down under."

For the most part Australia has a regular coastline. Only the Gulf of Carpentaria in the north and the Great Australian Bight in the south cut deeply into the land. The Great Barrier Reef, the longest coral reef in the world, stretches for 1,250 miles (2,012 kilometers) off the northeast coast. Actually the reef is made up of many reefs and small islands.

A few miles inland from the east coast is an area of low mountain ranges and tablelands, known as the Eastern Highlands, or the Great Dividing Range. These ranges divide the heavily populated coastal plains from the less populated plains of the interior. Most of Australia's industry is located in the eastern coastal plains. The Eastern Highlands are low, with most of them under 3,000 feet (910 meters) above sea level. The mountains in the more rugged southeastern section are somewhat higher. Mt. Kosciusko, Australia's highest point, is found here. The island of Tasmania, 150 miles (240 kilometers) to the southeast, is a continuation of these highlands.

A second major region, the Central Lowlands, covers about one-third of the continent. It extends from the Gulf of Carpentaria in the north to the eastern shore of the Great Australian Bight in the south. Scientists think that these lowlands were once covered with water. Beneath the lowlands are several artesian basins—areas of underground water. One of them, the Great Artesian Basin, underlies about one-fifth of Australia and is the largest artesian basin in the world. The water cannot be used for continuous irrigation, but it does provide water for cattle and sheep. Much of this region is dry but there are large areas of grassland in the east. The Murray-Darling river system in the southeastern part of the region is the major river system in Australia. There are several large irrigation projects along the rivers. Their valleys are among the most productive farming and grazing areas in the country. Although the Australian economy is highly industrialized, livestock is an important part of the economy.

A third region, the Western Plateau, is in the western two-thirds of the continent. It is an area of desert and semidesert land. Most of the plateau is below 1,000 feet (305 meters) above sea level. Three very large deserts—the Gibson, Great Sandy, and Great Victoria deserts—are located here. The plateau is rimmed by steep cliffs, except in a few areas where it drops gently to the sea. In the south, the Nullarbor Plain is an unusual area below the cliffs. It is a remarkable smooth, barren lowland riddled by numerous underground caves. The rest of the plateau is edged by a narrow coastal plain. Although most of the Western Plateau is not suited to agriculture, it is rich in minerals.

Australia's climate is generally mild throughout the year. Although there is a rainy season from January to about April, most of the continent does not receive enough rain. Parts of it receive less than 10 inches (25 centimeters) a year. One of the striking things about Australia's weather is its changeability, especially in the south. For a short time each year, the winds will abruptly change direction, temperatures will rise or fall, or it will suddenly rain or stop raining.

Because so much of the interior is dry, most of Australia's major cities are located along the coast. Much of the transportation between cities is by ship, and all of the state capitals are seaports.

New Zealand is situated about 1,200 miles (1,930 kilometers) southeast of Australia. The nation has two main islands, North Island and South Island.

New Zealand is a mountainous country known for its beautiful scenery. North Island is of volcanic origin and some of its volcanoes are still active. The hills are covered with forests, but many of them have been cut down. North Island also has many hot springs, boiling mud, geysers, lakes of different colors, and waterfalls. A high mountain range called the Southern Alps runs along most of the length of South Island. Much of the land is fertile and is used for growing crops and raising sheep and cattle. Most of the cattle are found on North Island and the sheep on South Island.

New Zealand has several rivers but few are long or deep enough to be used for transportation. They are used for water power, however.

The climate of New Zealand is temperate, with mild winters and warm summers. It is warmest in the north and it gets increasingly colder to the south. Temperatures are lower at higher altitudes. Rainfall is heavy in most areas, especially on the west coast of South Island, where it sometimes reaches 250 inches (635 centimeters) a year in parts of the Southern Alps.

1. What is the Great Barrier Reef?
2. What are the three major land regions of Australia?
3. What is the Great Dividing Range?
4. Why is the Murray-Darling river system the most important drainage system in the country?
5. What large islands make up the nation of New Zealand?
6. Why do you think the climate of New Zealand is warmest in the north and colder to the south?

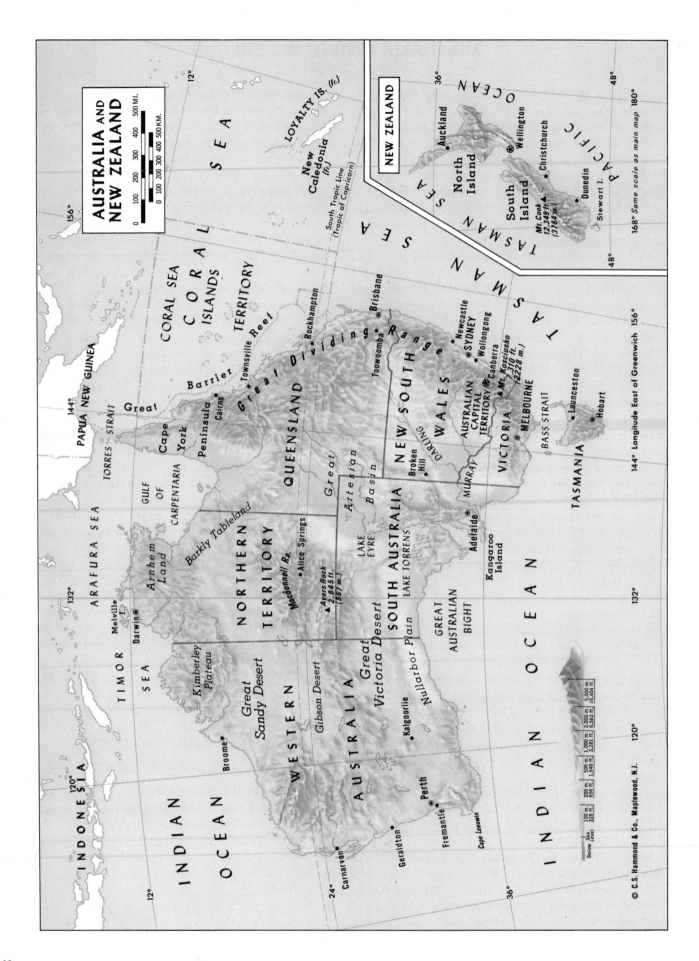

AUSTRALIA AND
NEW ZEALAND

500 MI.
0 100 200 300 400
0 100 200 300 400 500 KM.

NEW ZEALAND

168° Same scale as main map 180°

PACIFIC OCEAN

Auckland
North
Island
Wellington
South
Island
Christchurch
Mt. Cook
12,349 ft.
(3764 m.)
Dunedin
Stewart I.

TASMAN SEA

CORAL SEA

CORAL SEA ISLANDS TERRITORY

LOYALTY IS. (Fr.)

New
Caledonia
(Fr.)

South Tropic Line
(Tropic of Capricorn)

156°

12°

PAPUA NEW GUINEA

INDONESIA 120°

ARAFURA SEA

TIMOR SEA

Melville I.
Darwin

Arnhem
Land

Kimberley
Plateau

Broome

Great
Sandy Desert

Gibson Desert

WESTERN
AUSTRALIA

Great
Victoria Desert

Kalgoorlie

Geraldton

Perth

Fremantle

Cape Leeuwin

INDIAN OCEAN

INDIAN OCEAN

Carnarvon

GULF
OF
CARPENTARIA

TORRES STRAIT

Cape
York
Peninsula

Barrier

Great

Cairns

Townsville Reef

Rockhampton

Great Dividing Range

Barkly Tableland

NORTHERN
TERRITORY

Alice Springs

Macdonnell Ra.

Ayers Rock
2,845 ft.
(867 m.)

QUEENSLAND

Great
Artesian
Basin

LAKE
EYRE

LAKE TORRENS

SOUTH AUSTRALIA

Nullarbor Plain

GREAT
AUSTRALIAN
BIGHT

Toowoomba

Brisbane

DARLING

Broken
Hill

NEW SOUTH
WALES

Newcastle
SYDNEY
Wollongong
Canberra
AUSTRALIAN
CAPITAL
TERRITORY
Mt. Kosciusko
7,310 ft.
(2228 m.)

MURRAY

VICTORIA

MELBOURNE

Adelaide

Kangaroo
Island

Launceston

Hobart

TASMANIA

BASS STRAIT

TASMAN SEA

INDIAN OCEAN

156° Longitude East of Greenwich

144° Longitude East of Greenwich

132°

120°

36°

24°

12°

Sea
Level
Below

100 m.
328 ft.

200 m.
656 ft.

500 m.
1,640 ft.

1,000 m.
3,281 ft.

2,000 m.
6,562 ft.

5,000 m.
16,404 ft.

© C.S. Hammond & Co., Maplewood, N.J.

36°

48°

68

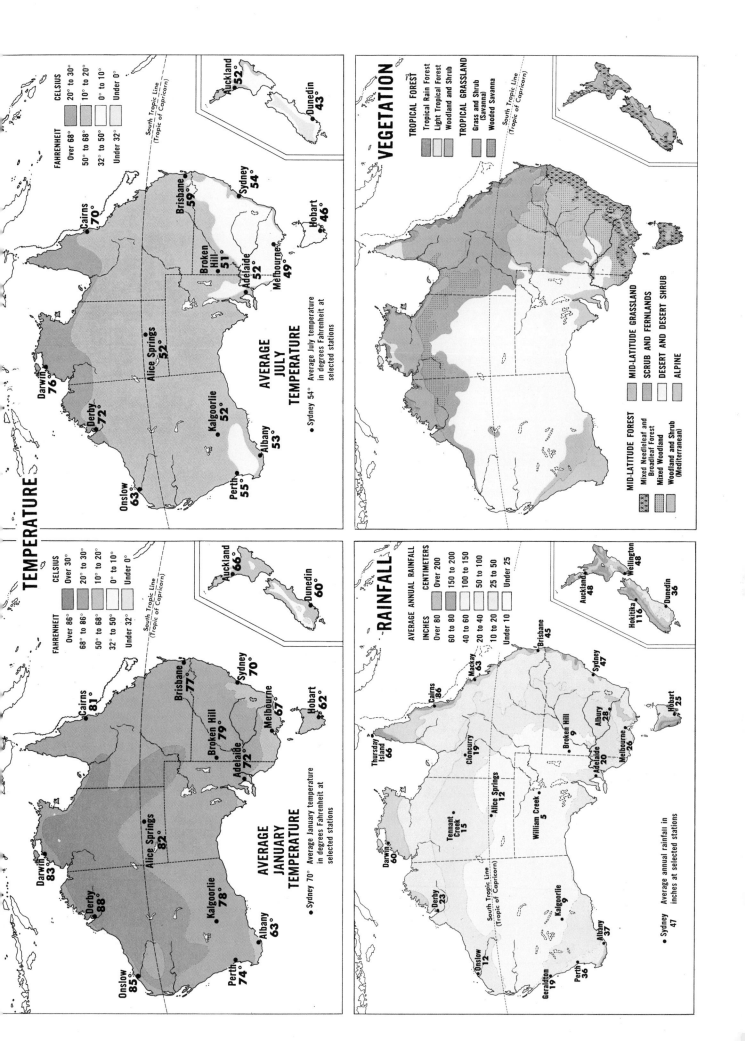

TEMPERATURE

AVERAGE JANUARY TEMPERATURE

FAHRENHEIT	CELSIUS
Over 86°	Over 30°
68° to 86°	20° to 30°
50° to 68°	10° to 20°
32° to 50°	0° to 10°
Under 32°	Under 0°

South Tropic Line
(Tropic of Capricorn)

Onslow 85°
Darwin 83°
Derby 88°
Kalgoorlie 78°
Albany 63°
Perth 74°
Alice Springs 82°
Broken Hill 79°
Adelaide 72°
Melbourne 67°
Hobart 62°
Sydney 70°
Brisbane 77°
Cairns 81°

Auckland 66°
Dunedin 60°

● Sydney 70° Average January temperature in degrees Fahrenheit at selected stations

TEMPERATURE

AVERAGE JULY TEMPERATURE

FAHRENHEIT	CELSIUS
Over 68°	20° to 30°
50° to 68°	10° to 20°
32° to 50°	0° to 10°
Under 32°	Under 0°

South Tropic Line
(Tropic of Capricorn)

Onslow 63°
Darwin 76°
Derby 72°
Kalgoorlie 52°
Albany 53°
Perth 55°
Alice Springs 52°
Broken Hill 51°
Adelaide 52°
Melbourne 49°
Hobart 46°
Sydney 54°
Brisbane 59°
Cairns 70°

Auckland 52°
Dunedin 43°

● Sydney 54° Average July temperature in degrees Fahrenheit at selected stations

RAINFALL

AVERAGE ANNUAL RAINFALL

INCHES	CENTIMETERS
Over 80	Over 200
60 to 80	150 to 200
40 to 60	100 to 150
20 to 40	50 to 100
10 to 20	25 to 50
Under 10	Under 25

South Tropic Line
(Tropic of Capricorn)

Onslow 12
Derby 23
Darwin 60
Geraldton 19
Perth 36
Albany 37
Kalgoorlie 9
Tennant Creek 15
Alice Springs 12
William Creek 5
Cloncurry 19
Thursday Island 66
Cairns 86
Mackay 63
Brisbane 45
Broken Hill 9
Adelaide 20
Melbourne 26
Albury 28
Sydney 47
Hobart 25

Auckland 48
Hokitika 116
Wellington 48
Dunedin 36

● Sydney 47 Average annual rainfall in inches at selected stations

VEGETATION

TROPICAL FOREST
- Tropical Rain Forest
- Light Tropical Forest
- Woodland and Shrub

TROPICAL GRASSLAND
- Grass and Shrub (Savanna)
- Wooded Savanna

MID-LATITUDE FOREST
- Mixed Needleleaf and Broadleaf Forest
- Mixed Woodland
- Woodland and Shrub (Mediterranean)

MID-LATITUDE GRASSLAND
- SCRUB AND FERNLANDS
- DESERT AND DESERT SHRUB
- ALPINE

South Tropic Line
(Tropic of Capricorn)

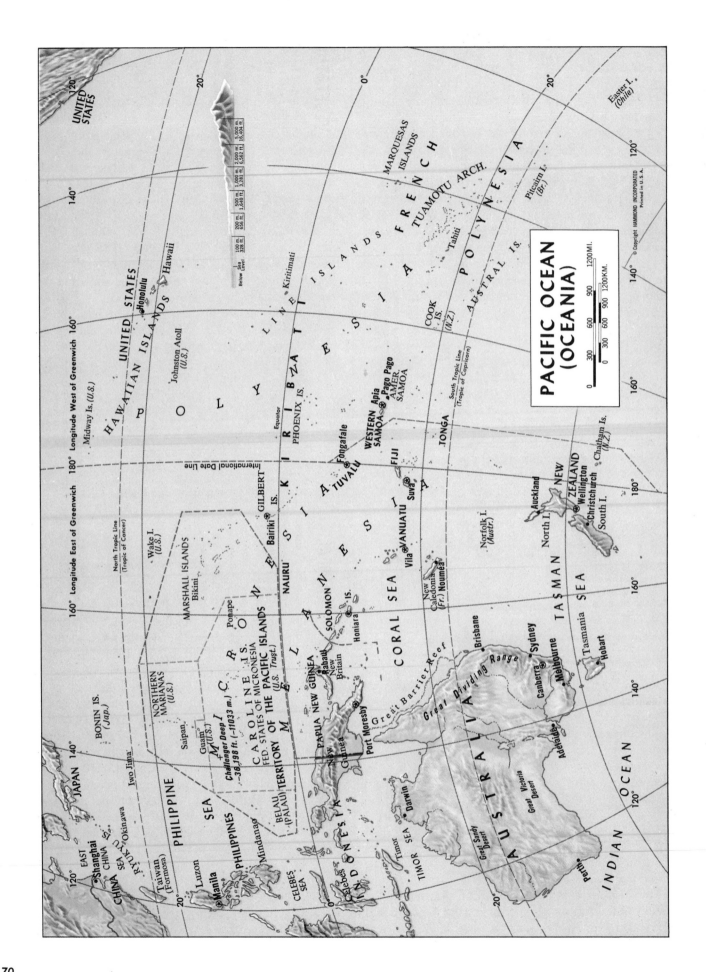

PACIFIC OCEAN
(OCEANIA)

© Copyright HAMMOND INCORPORATED
Printed in U.S.A.

70

OCEANIA

Oceania is the name of the 25,000 or more islands scattered across the Pacific Ocean. Some of the islands are little more than bits of rocks and sand. Others are much larger and are crowded with people. The people of Oceania speak many different languages. Until recently they lived isolated from the rest of the world.

The islands of Oceania were formed in two ways. Some are the result of erupting volcanoes. Flowing lava cooled around the volcanoes and built up land. Because volcanic soil is fertile, the mountainous or hilly lands of these islands are covered with trees and other plant life. The other kind of Pacific island was formed by the piling up of coral until a reef of land was formed. These coral reefs usually enclose a body of water, called a *lagoon,* in the center. Such coral islands are called *atolls*. They are low-lying islands with poor soil.

The Pacific islands are often divided into three groups — Polynesia, Micronesia, and Melanesia. The largest of the groups is Polynesia. The word "Polynesia" means "many islands." This group is in the shape of a huge triangle in the central Pacific. The southwestern corner of the triangle is at New Zealand. Its western boundary extends northward through the Tonga Islands and along the International Date Line to Midway Island. The boundary then runs southeast through the Hawaiian Islands to its point at Easter Island. From there it turns back to New Zealand. Most of the islands of Polynesia are mountainous and covered with thick forests.

Micronesia means "small islands." This group lies in the western Pacific between the equator and Japan. They stretch from the Philippines eastward to Polynesia. Micronesia includes the Mariana, Caroline, Marshall, Gilbert (Kiribati), and Ellice (Tuvalu) islands. Most are volcanic islands.

The third group, Melanesia, is just south of Micronesia. Melanesia means "black islands." These islands lie northeast of Australia and extend from New Guinea eastward to the Fiji Islands. The Melanesian islands are mostly mountainous and heavily forested.

Since most of Oceania is within the tropics, the climate of the region is hot and humid. The heat is made bearable, however, by cool ocean breezes. There is little change in season, and the year is divided into periods of greater and lesser rainfall.

A few islands, such as New Caledonia, Fiji, and the New Hebrides (Vanuatu), have rich mineral resources. On all, agriculture provides a living for its inhabitants.

1. What is another name for the Pacific Islands?
2. What are the three main island groups?
3. What is an atoll?

ANTARCTICA MAP—PAGE 72

Antarctica is the huge continent covered with ice and snow that surrounds the South Pole. Over the centuries the ice and snow have built up over the land until they cover about 95 percent of it. This giant mass of ice has made Antarctica the highest continent, with its general elevation around 7,500 feet (2,286 meters) above sea level. This ice also covers most of the coastline and in some places extends into the ocean, forming huge shelves of ice.

Antarctica is roughly circular in shape. Only the Weddell Sea and the Ross Sea extend any distance inland. Most of the continent is a plateau. The Transantarctic Mountains, a series of ranges running from Victoria Land to Coats Land, divide the continent into two regions—the East Antarctic and the West Antarctic.

East Antarctica, that portion south of the Indian Ocean and facing Africa and Australia, is the larger of the two regions. It is a high plateau that is one of the world's driest areas. West Antarctica, facing South America and the Pacific Ocean, is made up of a series of mountain ranges. One part of this region, the Antarctic Peninsula, is a long, mountainous ridge that stretches northward toward South America for about 1,200 miles (1,930 kilometers). The peninsula resembles the Andes and is probably part of the same mountain chain. If the ice were to melt, the peninsula would be seen to resemble southern Chile and to have many islands and deep fiords. Many of the peaks that can be seen above the ice cap are volcanoes, and at least two of them are still active. Vinson Massif, 16,864 feet (5,140 meters) above sea level is the continent's highest point.

Antarctica is the coldest, windiest, and the most barren of all the continents. No trees grow here. In only a few places will a few plants grow for a very short period of time each year.

1. Describe the two regions of Antarctica.
2. Name four countries that have stations in Antarctica.

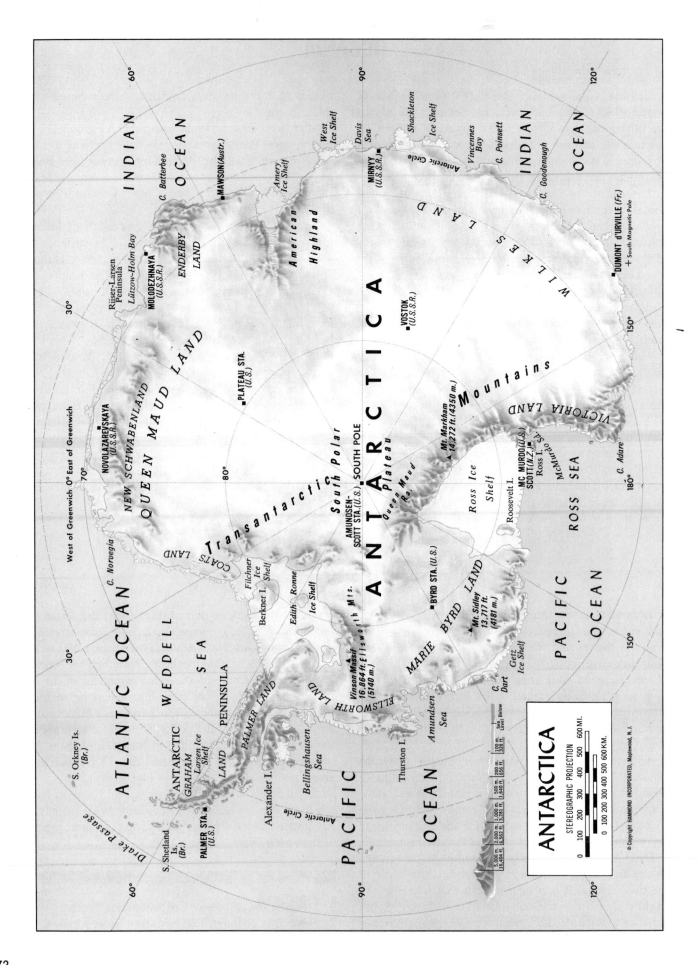

INDIAN

OCEAN

C. Batterbee

MAWSON *(Austr.)*

West
Ice Shelf

Davis
Sea

Shackleton
Ice Shelf

Vincennes
Bay

C. Poinsett

C. Goodenough

INDIAN

OCEAN

MIRNYY
(U.S.S.R.)

Antarctic Circle

DUMONT d'URVILLE *(Fr.)*

+ South Magnetic Pole

Amery
Ice Shelf

ENDERBY

LAND

Rüiser-Larsen
Peninsula

Lützow-Holm Bay

MOLODEZHNAYA
(U.S.S.R.)

American

Highland

W I L K E S   L A N D

VOSTOK
(U.S.S.R.)

A T L A N T I C   O C E A N

West of Greenwich   0° East of Greenwich

30°

NOVOLAZAREVSKAYA
(U.S.S.R.)

NEW SCHWABENLAND

Q U E E N   M A U D   L A N D

PLATEAU STA.
(U.S.)

A N T A R C T I C A

Mountains

VICTORIA LAND

Mt. Markham
14,272 ft. (4350 m.)

South Polar

Plateau

Queen Maud Ra.

SOUTH POLE

AMUNDSEN-
SCOTT STA.*(U.S.)*

C. Norvegia

COATS   LAND

Transantarctic

Filchner
Ice
Shelf

Berkner I.

Edith Ronne
Ice Shelf

Ellsworth Mts.

Ross Ice
Shelf

MC MURDO*(U.S.)*
SCOTT*(N.Z.)*

McMurdo Sd.

Ross I.

C. Adare

180°

R O S S

S E A

WEDDELL

SEA

BYRD STA. *(U.S.)*

MARIE   BYRD   LAND

Mt. Sidley
13,717 ft.
(4181 m.)

Roosevelt I.

Getz
Ice Shelf

P A C I F I C

O C E A N

150°

S. Orkney Is.
(Br.)

Drake Passage

S. Shetland
Is.
(Br.)

PALMER STA.
(U.S.)

ANTARCTIC

GRAHAM

LAND

Larsen Ice
Shelf

PALMER LAND

Alexander I.

Bellingshausen
Sea

Antarctic Circle

Thurston I.

Amundsen
Sea

ELLSWORTH LAND

Vinson Massif
16,864 ft.
(5140 m.)

C.
Dart

P A C I F I C

O C E A N

90°

120°

60°

90°

120°

150°

60°

30°

70°

80°

Sea Below
Level

100 m.
328 ft.

200 m.
656 ft.

500 m.
1,640 ft.

1,000 m.
3,281 ft.

2,000 m.
6,562 ft.

5,000 m.
16,404 ft.

ANTARCTICA

STEREOGRAPHIC PROJECTION

100   200   300   400   500   600 MI.

0   100   200   300   400   500   600 KM.

© Copyright HAMMOND INCORPORATED, Maplewood, N.J.

GLOSSARY OF ABBREVIATIONS

A

Afgh., Afghan. — Afghanistan
Afr. — Africa
Ala. — Alabama
Alb. — Albania
Alg. — Algeria
Alta. — Alberta
Amer. Samoa —American Samoa
arch. — archipelago
Arg. — Argentina
Ariz. — Arizona
Ark. — Arkansas
Arm. S. S. R. — Armenian Soviet
   Socialist Republic
Aust., Austr. — Australia
Azer. S. S. R. — Azerbaidzhan
   Soviet Socialist Republic

B

Bah. — Bahrain
Bang. — Bangladesh
Barb. — Barbados
Belg. — Belgium
Ben. — Benin
Bh. — Bhutan
Bol. — Bolivia
Bots. — Botswana
Braz. — Brazil
Br. — British
Br. Ind. Oc. Terr. — British
   Indian Ocean Territory
Bulg. — Bulgaria

C

c. — cape
Calif. — California
Cam. — Cameroon
Camb. — Cambodia
cap. — capital
Cent. Afr. Rep. — Central African
   Republic
chan. — channel
Col. — Colombia
Colo. — Colorado
Conn. — Connecticut
C. R. — Costa Rica
Czech. — Czechoslovakia

D

Del. — Delaware
Den. — Denmark
des. — desert
Dom. Rep. — Dominican Republic

E

E. Ger. — East Germany
Ec. — Ecuador
El. Sal. — El Salvador
Eng. — England
est. — estuary
Est. S. S. R. — Estonian Soviet
   Socialist Republic
Eth. — Ethiopia
Eur. — Europe

F

Fla. — Florida
Fr. — France, French
Fr. Gu. — French Guiana
Ft. — Fort

G

Ga. — Georgia
Gamb. — Gambia
Ger. — Germany
Gr. — Greece
Gren. — Grenada
Guat. — Guatemala
Gui.-Bis. — Guinea-Bissau
Guy. — Guyana

H

Hond. — Honduras
Hung. — Hungary

I

i., isl. — island
I. C. — Ivory Coast
Ice. — Iceland
Ill. — Illinois
Ind. — Indiana
Indon. — Indonesia
Ire. — Ireland
is., isls. — islands
Isr. — Israel
It. — Italy, Italian

J

Jam. — Jamaica
Jap. — Japan, Japanese
Jor. — Jordan

K

Kans. — Kansas
Ky. — Kentucky

L

l. — lake
La. — Louisiana
Lat. S. S. R. — Latvian Soviet
   Socialist Republic
Liech. — Liechtenstein
Lith. S. S. R. — Lithuanian Soviet
   Socialist Republic
Lux. — Luxembourg

M

Mal. — Malawi
Man. — Manitoba
Mass. — Massachusetts
Maur. — Mauritania
Md. — Maryland
Mex. — Mexico
Mich. — Michigan
Minn. — Minnesota
Miss. — Mississippi
Mo. — Missouri
Mold. S. S. R. — Moldavian Soviet
   Socialist Republic
Mont. — Montana
Mor. — Morocco
Moz. — Mozambique
mt., mte. — mount
mts. — mountains

N

N. Amer. — North America
nat'l — national
N. B. — New Brunswick
N. C. — North Carolina
N. Cal. — New Caledonia
N. Dak. — North Dakota
Nebr. — Nebraska
Neth. — Netherlands
Neth. Ant. — Netherlands Antilles
Nev. — Nevada
Newf. — Newfoundland
N. H. — New Hampshire
Nic. — Nicaragua
Nig. — Nigeria
N. Ire. — Northern Ireland
N. J. — New Jersey
N. Kor. — North Korea
N. Mex. — New Mexico
N. S. — Nova Scotia
N. S. W. — New South Wales
N. Terr. — Northern Territories
N. W. T. — Northwest Territories
N. Y. — New York
N. Z. — New Zealand

O

Okla. — Oklahoma
Ont. — Ontario
Oreg. — Oregon

P

Pa. — Pennsylvania
Pak. — Pakistan
Pan. — Panama

Par. — Paraguay
P. D. R. Yemen — Peoples Democratic
   Republic of Yemen
P. E. I. — Prince Edward Island
pen. — peninsula
Phil. — Philippines
plat. — plateau
Pol. — Poland
Port. — Portugal, Portuguese
P. R. — Puerto Rico
pt., pte. — point

Q

Que. — Québec
Queens. — Queensland

R

r., riv. — river
ra. — range
reg. — region
rep. — republic
res. — reservoir
R. I. — Rhode Island
Rom. — Romania

S

sa. — serra, sierra
S. Afr. — South Africa
S. Amer. — South America
Sask. — Saskatchewan
Saudi Ar. — Saudi Arabia
S. C. — South Carolina
Scot. — Scotland
sd. — sound
S. Dak. — South Dakota
Sen. — Senegal
S. Kor. — South Korea
Sp. — Spain, Spanish
sprs. — springs
st., ste. — saint, sainte
sta. — station
str. — strait
Sur. — Suriname
Swaz. — Swaziland
Switz. — Switzerland
Syr. — Syria

T

Tan. — Tanzania
Tenn. — Tennessee
terr. — territory
Thai. — Thailand
Trin. & Tob. — Trinidad and
   Tobago
Tun. — Tunisia
Turk. — Turkey

U

U. A. E. — United Arab Emirates
U. K. — United Kingdom
un. — united
Urug. — Uruguay
U. S. — United States
U. S. S. R. — Union of Soviet
   Socialist Republics

V

Va. — Virginia
Ven. — Venezuela
Vic. — Victoria
vol. — volcano
Vt. — Vermont

W

Wash. — Washington
W. Ger. — West Germany
W. I. — West Indies
Wis. — Wisconsin
W. Samoa — Western Samoa
W. Va. — West Virginia
Wyo. — Wyoming

Y

Yugo. — Yugoslavia

Z

Zim. — Zimbabwe

Country	Area Sq. Mi.	Sq. Km.	Population	Page Ref.
*Afghanistan	250,775	649,507	16,363,000	61
Africa	11,707,000	30,321,130	484,000,000	33
Alabama, U.S.A.	51,705	133,916	3,893,978	15
Alaska, U.S.A.	591,004	1,530,700	401,851	20
*Albania	11,100	28,749	2,590,600	51
Alberta, Canada	255,285	661,185	2,237,724	11
*Algeria	919,591	2,381,740	18,666,000	35
Andorra	188	487	39,940	47
*Angola	481,351	1,246,700	7,262,000	38
Antarctica	5,500,000	14,245,000	....	72
*Antigua and Barbuda	171	443	75,000	24
*Argentina	1,072,070	2,776,661	28,438,000	31
Arizona, U.S.A.	114,000	295,260	2,718,425	19
Arkansas, U.S.A.	53,187	137,754	2,286,419	17
Asia	17,128,500	44,362,815	2,688,000,000	55
*Australia	2,966,136	7,682,300	14,576,330	68
*Austria	32,375	83,851	7,555,338	50
*Bahamas	5,382	13,939	209,505	24
*Bahrain	240	622	358,857	57
*Bangladesh	55,126	142,776	87,052,024	61
*Barbados	166	430	248,983	24
*Belgium	11,781	30,513	9,848,647	45
*Belize	8,867	22,966	145,353	22
*Benin	43,483	112,620	3,338,240	35
Bermuda	21	54	67,761	9
*Bhutan	18,147	47,000	1,301,000	61
*Bolivia	424,163	1,098,582	5,755,000	30
*Botswana	224,764	582,139	936,600	38
*Brazil	3,284,426	8,506,663	119,098,992	30
British Columbia, Canada..	366,253	948,596	2,744,467	11
Brunei	2,226	5,765	192,832	64
*Bulgaria	42,823	110,912	8,890,000	51
*Burkina Faso	105,869	274,200	7,094,000	35
*Burma	261,789	678,034	33,640,000	65
*Burundi	10,747	27,835	4,028,420	37
*Byelorussian S.S.R. (White Russian S.S.R.), U.S.S.R..	80,154	207,600	9,560,543	53
California, U.S.A.	158,706	411,049	23,667,837	19
*Cambodia (Kampuchea)	69,898	181,036	5,756,141	65
*Cameroon	183,568	475,441	8,503,000	37
*Canada	3,851,787	9,976,139	24,343,181	11
*Cape Verde	1,557	4,033	296,093	33
*Central African Republic...	242,000	626,780	2,284,000	37
Central America	197,480	511,475	22,000,000	22
*Chad	495,752	1,283,998	4,309,000	36
*Chile	292,257	756,946	11,275,440	31
*China, People's Rep. of....	3,691,000	9,559,690	1,008,175,288	62
China, Republic of (Taiwan)	13,971	36,185	18,029,798	62
*Colombia	439,513	1,138,339	28,776,000	28
Colorado, U.S.A.	104,091	269,596	2,889,735	19
*Comoros	719	1,862	345,000	33
*Congo	132,046	342,000	1,537,000	37
Connecticut, U.S.A.	5,018	12,997	3,107,576	13
*Costa Rica	19,575	50,700	2,271,000	22
*Cuba	44,206	114,494	9,706,369	24
*Cyprus	3,473	8,995	637,000	58
*Czechoslovakia	49,373	127,876	15,364,000	50
Delaware, U.S.A.	2,044	5,294	594,317	14
*Denmark	16,629	43,069	5,118,000	43
District of Columbia, U.S.A..	69	179	638,432	14
*Djibouti	8,880	23,000	386,000	36
*Dominica	290	751	74,089	24
*Dominican Republic	18,704	48,443	5,647,977	24
*Ecuador	109,483	283,561	8,644,000	29
*Egypt	386,659	1,001,447	43,465,000	36
*El Salvador	8,260	21,393	4,748,000	22
England, U.K.	50,516	130,836	46,220,995	42
*Equatorial Guinea	10,831	28,052	244,000	37
Estonian S.S.R., U.S.S.R....	17,413	45,100	1,466,000	53
*Ethiopia	471,776	1,221,900	31,065,000	36
Europe	4,057,000	10,507,630	690,000,000	40

Country	Area Sq. Mi.	Sq. Km.	Population	Page Ref.
*Fiji	7,055	18,272	645,000	70
*Finland	130,128	337,032	4,812,150	43
Florida, U.S.A.	58,664	151,940	9,746,421	15
*France	210,038	543,998	54,334,871	46
French Guiana	35,135	91,000	73,022	28
French Polynesia	1,544	4,000	150,000	70
*Gabon	103,346	267,666	555,000	37
*Gambia	4,127	10,689	601,000	35
Georgia, U.S.A.	58,910	152,577	5,462,997	15
*Germany, East (German Democratic Republic)..	41,768	108,179	16,732,486	44
*Germany, West (Federal Republic)	95,985	248,601	61,546,101	44
*Ghana	92,099	238,536	11,450,000	35
Gibraltar	2.28	5.91	29,648	47
*Greece	50,944	131,945	9,740,417	51
Greenland	84,000	2,175,600	51,000	9
*Grenada	133	344	103,103	24
Guam	209	541	105,979	70
*Guatemala	42,042	108,889	6,043,559	22
*Guinea	94,925	245,856	5,143,284	35
*Guinea-Bissau	13,948	36,125	810,000	35
*Guyana	83,000	214,970	793,000	28
*Haiti	10,694	27,697	5,053,792	24
Hawaii, U.S.A.	6,471	16,760	964,691	20
*Honduras	43,277	112,087	3,955,000	22
Hong Kong	403	1,044	4,986,560	62
*Hungary	35,919	93,030	10,702,000	50
*Iceland	39,768	103,000	231,000	43
Idaho, U.S.A.	83,564	216,431	944,038	18
Illinois, U.S.A.	56,345	145,934	11,427,414	16
*India	1,269,339	3,287,588	685,184,692	61
Indiana, U.S.A.	36,185	93,719	5,490,260	16
*Indonesia	788,430	2,042,034	147,490,298	64
Iowa, U.S.A.	56,275	145,752	2,913,808	16
*Iran	636,293	1,648,000	37,447,000	60
*Iraq	172,476	446,713	12,767,000	60
*Ireland	27,136	70,282	3,443,405	42
*Israel	7,847	20,324	3,980,000	59
*Italy	116,303	301,225	56,243,935	48
*Ivory Coast	124,504	322,465	7,920,000	35
*Jamaica	4,411	11,424	2,184,000	24
*Japan	145,730	377,441	117,060,396	63
*Jordan	35,000	90,650	2,152,273	59
Kansas, U.S.A.	82,277	213,097	2,364,236	16
Kentucky, U.S.A.	40,409	104,659	3,660,257	15
*Kenya	224,960	582,646	15,327,061	37
Kiribati	291	754	56,213	70
Korea, North	46,540	120,539	18,317,000	63
Korea, South	38,175	98,873	37,448,836	63
*Kuwait	6,532	16,918	1,355,827	57
*Laos	91,428	236,800	3,811,000	65
Latvian S.S.R., U.S.S.R.	24,595	63,700	2,521,000	53
*Lebanon	4,015	10,399	2,688,000	58
*Lesotho	11,720	30,355	1,339,000	38
*Liberia	43,000	111,370	1,873,000	35
*Libya	679,358	1,759,537	3,096,000	36
Liechtenstein	61	158	25,220	49
Lithuanian S.S.R., U.S.S.R..	25,174	65,200	3,398,000	53
Louisiana, U.S.A.	47,752	123,678	4,206,098	17
*Luxembourg	999	2,587	364,606	45
*Madagascar	226,657	587,041	8,955,000	38
Maine, U.S.A.	33,265	86,156	1,125,030	13
*Malawi	45,747	118,485	6,123,000	38
Malaya, Malaysia	50,806	131,588	11,138,227	65
*Malaysia	128,308	332,318	13,435,588	64
*Maldives	115	298	157,000	55